quilted panels
IN black & white

quilted panels
in black & white

Easy Techniques for Using Fabric Panels and Large Prints

Kay M. Capps Cross

KRAUSE PUBLICATIONS
CINCINNATI, OHIO

14 13 12 11 10   5 4 3 2 1

DISTRIBUTED IN CANADA BY FRASER DIRECT
100 Armstrong Avenue
Georgetown, ON, Canada L7G 5S4
Tel: (905) 877-4411

DISTRIBUTED IN THE U.K. AND EUROPE BY DAVID & CHARLES
Brunel House, Newton Abbot, Devon, TQ12 4PU, England
Tel: (+44) 1626 323200, Fax: (+44) 1626 323319
Email: postmaster@davidandcharles.co.uk

DISTRIBUTED IN AUSTRALIA BY CAPRICORN LINK
P.O. Box 704, S. Windsor NSW, 2756 Australia
Tel: (02) 4577-3555

Library of Congress Cataloging in Publication Data
Cross, Kay M. Capps.
  Quilted panels in black & white : easy techniques for using fabric panels and large prints / Kay M. Capps Cross.
       p. cm.
  Includes index.
  ISBN 978-1-4402-1133-1 (alk. paper)
  1. Patchwork--Patterns. 2. Quilting--Patterns. 3. Black in art. 4. White in art. I. Title.
  TT835.C74896 2010
  746.46'041--dc22
                        2010008610

Designer: Geoff Raker

Production coordinator: Greg Nock

Photographer: Al Parrish

Stylist: Lauren Emmerling

fw
media
www.fwmedia.com

Metric Conversion Chart

To convert	to	multiply by
Inches	Centimeters	2.54
Centimeters	Inches	0.4
Feet	Centimeters	30.5
Centimeters	Feet	0.03
Yards	Meters	0.9
Meters	Yards	1.1

Dedication

This book is dedicated to fabric-aholics everywhere. You know who you are, I know who you are and we are lucky to be who we are.

I cannot offer you a twelve-step program, but what I can offer you is a book with oodles of ideas for utilizing those panels you bought years ago that are still stuffed in the back of your closet. Dig them out, rev up your sewing machine and let's get quilting!

Acknowledgments

I would like to thank:

F+W Media for allowing me to create, write and share my ideas with you.

All the individuals at F+W that had a hand in showcasing my work. I so appreciate that you "get me" and celebrate the quilts in such a striking way.

Baby Lock "For the Love."

Bali Batiks, Inc.; Island Batiks, Inc.; Marcus Brothers; Red Rooster Fabrics; Avlyn; Exclusively Quilters and Northcott Silks; Lyndhurst Studios and Andover Fabrics for supplying me with inspirational fabrics.

My four incredible children for their patience, adaptability, character and daily inspiration. I am thankful each day that I get to live with them.

My He-man for providing house, home, a studio large enough to store lots of wonderful fabric and mostly for creating a family with me.

My goddesses, my friends and my students for encouraging, teaching and supporting me.

The quilting world for recognizing that there is beauty and value in all types of quilting—even when it is wonky!

My Grandma Angels for visiting me and reminding me they are never far away.

Contents

Introduction

In an effort to go green like the rest of the country, I went digging through my old totes of fabric for inspiration. In the recesses were many, many panel pieces for dollhouses, books, aprons and many other things already printed and ready to sew together. Not only can I now make all these items, but I can also buy new, high-quality, interesting and artistic panels from almost all the manufacturers of quilting fabric. This book is an effort to give you inspiration—to find uses for all those beautiful new panels now available and also for those panels that have been hidden in the back of the closet for years. Whether kitschy, fun, memorable or just wacky, these panels can star in all types of quilts. They can be layered on a baby quilt, a full-sized quilt or incorporated in any type quilt you want. This book will offer you ideas in different sizes—utilizing different techniques—and will help you reduce that stash!

I knew the walrus panel was going to come in handy some day. I also thought the adorable *Little Orphan Annie* pillow panel would make something terrific. I just didn't know when, where or how. With this book you will be able to unearth those hidden treasures, and you will know what to do with them. Bring out the tubs from the closet!

Using a few simple formulas, traditional techniques and some contemporary techniques too, you will be able to find an application for any of the panels you have unearthed.

We've seen those new panels that just need a border or two slapped on to make them ready to quilt. While that may be the best option for some panels, there are also a few things we can do to enhance them and create unique works of art, while maintaining the simplicity and speed of working with preprinted panels.

There are design principles and formulas that can help quilters determine how best to use panels of a certain size; for instance, I'm including the Fibonacci numbers, which are wonderful design tools if you know how to use them. But what I rely on most is my inner design sense. My eye tells me if I like the balance of a piece or if something is off. If an individual block or fabric reaches out and grabs me, I adjust it. If the piece as a whole grabs me, I have done my work.

Along the way, I'll pass along some tidbits I have learned from my elementary and high school art teacher, through trial and error, and things that just make sense to me. Whether you decide to follow the mathematical or inner-voice route to design, either one is going to help you get the results you desire. Simple tools and ideas, along with a bit of inspiration, will get you moving toward emptying out those bins of preprinted panels and things you were just about ready to purge. Hold off long enough to get through this book. You will find out how to turn those oldies, and some great new pieces, into treasures.

SECTION 1
The Basics

Quilting "basics" are approached in different ways by different quilters. I prefer a "try it all and see what works" approach. Throughout my quilting life I have amassed many gadgets and experimented with a wide variety of techniques. I don't claim to be an expert, so I'll tell you right up front that the material presented in the first section is not the only way, or even the best way, to do things. It is just the way I do things. I try to find the easiest way to get through the cutting and stitching so that I can see what develops. Perhaps I cut corners, perhaps I don't iron as often as others do—but I enjoy the process and that is what is important to me.

Having said all of that, I will present some guidelines and basic techniques that I use. These basic ideas will get you started quilting and help you decipher the potentially confusing jargon of quilters. The information will take you from fabric selection all the way to binding your quilt. If you are an accomplished quilter already, go ahead and jump to the projects on page 28! Otherwise, take your time and check out the tools that I think work really well, some basic quilting information and lingo, along with some time-saving tips.

Selecting Fabrics

Here we are at one of my favorite topics and activities—fabric selection! Shopping is one of the most important steps when I am designing. Not only do I love fondling fabric, but I'm a lazy quilter as well, so if I shop carefully, I have much less work to do later because the fabric does the work for me.

There are three basic things I look for when selecting my fabrics: scale, value and contrast.

Scale

Scale is the size of the design on the cloth. Using designs that are all the same scale in a quilt will make it lie calm and flat. It may make a very beautiful, homogenous quilt, but it will most likely be lacking in excitement. Scale variation adds character and interest to a quilt. I love to find fabrics with various spacing of the motifs because that creates a noticeable splash in the fabric pool.

Value

Value is how light or dark a fabric is. Value is completely relative, depending on the choices in each quilt. The widest range will pack the most punch. The fabric print also plays a role in value. The more widely spaced a motif, the more background shows through.

To help you categorize fabrics by value, just squint when viewing them. This helps blur the fabric, making it easier to determine value. I just take my glasses off to get the right blur—it works great for me!

Contrast

Range of contrast is very much a personal decision with each quilt. Many quilters strive for blended and smooth quilts with no bumps or ridges to give away where a large contrast step exists. Others like a more defined look with greater contrast between fabrics. Still others like huge steps of contrast to punch up a quilt's design and shape.

Variety in Scale
When pulling fabrics together for a quilt, find pieces with big differences in scale. The pieces in this picture go from a very small scale to a very large scale with a fun and exciting loopy print in between.

A Range of Values
The wider the value range of your fabrics, the bolder your design.

The Role Prints Play
A fabric's print can determine its value. The more spacing there is between patterns, the more background you can see. This can swing the value to one side or the other.

Swaying the Value Pendulum

Very large prints can also sway the value pendulum in an unexpected way. For example, a large floral print on a black background won't be completely dark in value if the print is primarily white. The same is true of the reverse: A very large floral print on a white background won't be entirely light in value if the print is primarily dark.

Squinting to Determine Value

If you squint while viewing this fabric sample, you'll see much more white than black, so the value will be lighter than expected.

Using Contrast for Effect

Not only is a design amplified with high contrast, but the clarity and simplicity are celebrated as well. No murky lines or vague shapes appear in designs with very elevated jumps in value. High contrast equals high excitement!

Tools for the Job

We've shopped for fabric—now, what tools do we need? There are so many kinds of rulers, threads, scissors, cutting mats—you name it—it's enough to make your head spin! So what should you use? The key is to use what you need to make quilting more enjoyable.

Rulers

It can be daunting to maneuver through the vast array of rulers available. I use several brands that like for different reasons. Try different brands to find what works best for you and which markings you can see most clearly. The key is to avoid those rulers that slither away when touched with a blade and those that have confusing markings. Who needs the extra frustration or confusion? I, for one, supply enough of that myself!

Whatever you do, don't switch brands in the middle of a project. The markings and measurements can vary and be interpreted differently brand to brand. Little discrepancies like that can make a difference in your finished product.

Scissors and Rotary Cutters

I need scissors for paper, threads and fabric (and they have to fit my big thumbs).

I also need rotary cutters in different shapes and sizes to reduce fatigue (from continually using the same one), and to ensure I always have one close at hand. Remember, spare blades are must-have items for your rotary cutters. Better tools make for a better quilting experience.

Cutting Mats

Swiveling cutting mats make cutting, straightening and trimming a cinch. No more walking around to the other side of the table to cut!

Threads

High-quality thread is a must-have. I see no point in spending my time using lesser-quality threads when better ones exist and are readily available. Higher quality equals less breakage, less lint and more fun!

Pins and Pin Holders

Another essential is a magnetized pin holder. It is crucial for gathering the pins I knock over in my haste to grab the next stack of strips to piece!

Irons and Pressing Cloths

I do a lot of ironing right at my sewing machine, so I use an assortment of wooden or hand irons in addition to a good-quality iron. An appliqué pressing cloth is also a handy gadget to have.

Selecting the Right Tools
I use tools that make quilting easier, faster, more efficient, more accurate and, most importantly, enjoyable.

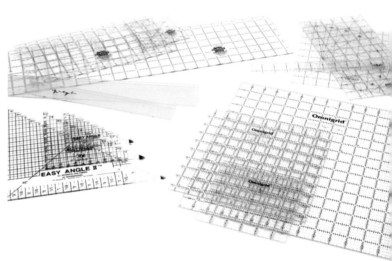

Rulers
I keep a variety of rulers on hand. One set, with yellow markings, is for dark fabrics so I can see the lines easier. Another set has grippers on the back side for cutting strips without slipping. The beautiful yellow rulers have a ridge for trimming ¼" seams effortlessly. I also have specialty rulers to cut triangles and trim off points. All of these allow piecing to be more enjoyable and quicker, making them very worthwhile purchases.

Batting

Variety is the key to my tool collection, and batting is no exception. I use an assortment of batting types for my quilts. Because I use very dark fabrics, I also use a black poly batting when my quilts are dark overall.

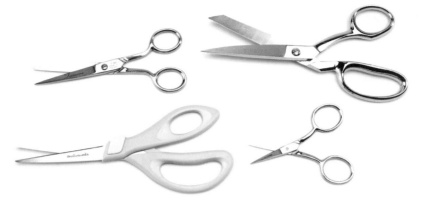

Scissors

It's important to have paper scissors, fabric scissors and thread scissors in your stash of essentials.

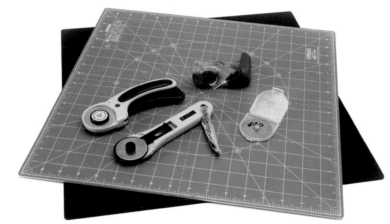

Rotary Cutters and Cutting Mats

Not only do I switch out my rotary cutter for comfort, I also go from cutter to cutter to find the sharpest blade. If that fails, I change the blade. To protect my table surface, I always make cuts on top of a self-healing mat.

Irons and Appliqué Pressing Cloths

I keep my ironing supplies near my sewing machine because pressing is an important part of the quilt-making process.

Batting

I enjoy playing with cotton and cotton blends for all-around trouble-free quilting. For beautiful drape and subtle texture, I use bamboo and silk batting. Wool batting is unbeatable for heightened detail without tremendous puff.

Terminology and Definitions

Sometimes we quilters assume that the terms we use are common knowledge. Having been a new quilter, I know that is not true. I don't want you to fumble around trying to figure out what I'm talking about, so I'm including a glossary of frequently used terms and descriptions. I hope this helps!

Selvage
The tighter woven edge of the fabric. The selvage does not stretch or behave like the rest of the fabric, so it should be removed and not used.

Lengthwise Grain
The grain running the length of the goods, parallel with the selvages. The fabric does not stretch or give when pulled in this direction.

Cross Grain
The grain of the fabric going across the goods from selvage to selvage. The fabric will stretch a bit in this direction.

¼" Seam Allowance
The measurement of the seam allowance on the outside of the stitching line.

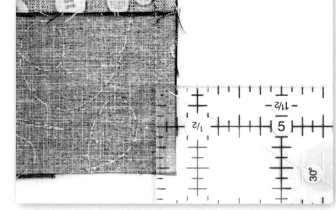

Half-Square Triangle
A triangle resulting from cutting a square in half once from corner to corner.

Quarter-Square Triangle
A triangle resulting from cutting a square in half twice from corner to corner.

Strip Piecing
Sewing together long strips of fabric cut widthwise (cross-grained) to make strip sets.

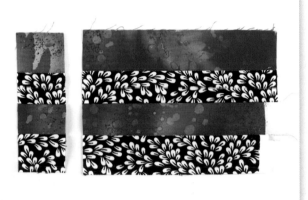

Subcutting
Cutting segments of strip sets already sewn together.

Matching or Nestling Seams
Setting seam lines right on top of another, right sides together, with the seam allowances going in opposite directions. Your fingers will learn how it feels when the joint is smooth with no gap or overlap.

Press, Don't Iron
Setting the iron down on the fabric to heat and flatten it, not pushing the iron back and forth. Pressing will flatten, but ironing may distort your pieces and fabric.

Setting the Seam
Pressing the seam allowance in the direction you want it to go before you press the fabrics or pieces open.

Press the Strips Open
Pressing at the seam, nudging the top fabric open over the seam allowance.

Bias Binding
Binding made of strips cut on the bias (45° angle from cross or straight grain), typically in 2¼" or 2½" widths. I use 2¼" strips. I often use bias binding with striped, checked or plaid fabric to create snazzy binding with the print angled for the binding.

Straight-Grained Binding
Binding made of strips cut cross grain (selvage to selvage), typically in 2¼" or 2½" widths. I use straight-grained binding with batik fabric that doesn't have a linear pattern, or with solid black fabric.

Chain Piecing
Sewing strip set after strip set, or piece after piece, without stopping or breaking the thread in between. This is a terrific speed technique.

Making Continuous Bias Binding

There is an easy method for making continuous bias binding instead of cutting strips and joining them all into one long strip. This system does everything at once.

1 Start with a large square of fabric. I use a chart—Quilter's Strip Ticket—to determine the size square I need. It is published by Lamb Art Press/Q Snap in Parsons, Tennessee.

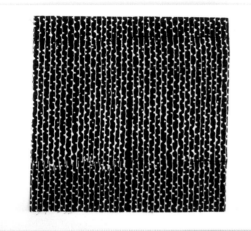

2 Cut the square in half, corner to corner.

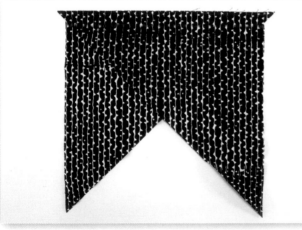

3 Layer the triangles right sides together to make a pair of pointy pants. Sew together with a ¼" seam.

4 Press the seam open. Now we have a parallelogram.

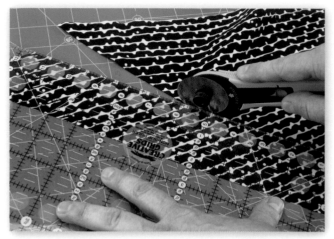

5 On one diagonal edge, begin cutting a starter strip in your desired width. I use 2¼" strips. Do not cut all the way across the fabric.

6 Flip out the starter strip and line up the straight edges right sides together. This will create a tube with the diagonal, or bias, on the outer edges.

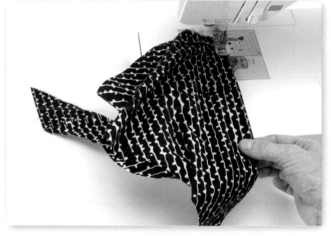

7 Sew the straight edges together with a ¼" seam.

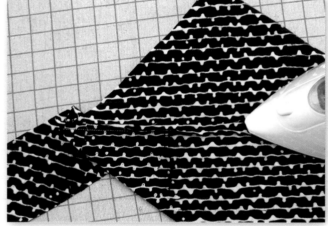

8 Press the seam open.

9 Put a small cutting mat inside the tube and continue cutting the strip around the tube to the end, starting at the starter strip. The spiral cutting creates a long bias strip.

10 Press the strip in half with wrong sides together. Roll it up and it is ready to use! Notice that the striped pattern is diagonal on the strip.

Making Straight-Grained Binding

Once upon a time, in a long ago quilt class, I was told that straight-grained binding was a no-no. This is not so-so. I have been happily and successfully using straight-grained binding with batiks and other fabrics since I got brave enough to break that rule! Cross-grained strips provide just a touch of stretch and are quite suitable if they don't have a print that is better suited to diagonal strips.

1 Cut cross-grained strips in your desired width. You will need enough length to go all the way around the quilt.

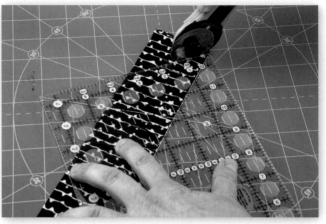

2 Cut each end of every strip at a 45° angle.

3 Piece the strips together by layering them, right sides together with the points extending, and sew.

4 Press all seams open and trim off all points.

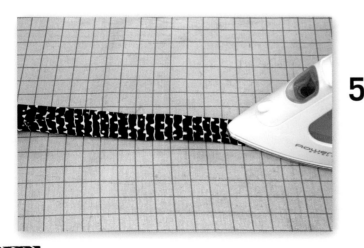

5 Press the long strip in half, wrong sides together. Notice how the strip design is perpendicular to the edge, as opposed to diagonal in the bias binding.

Rotary-Cutting Basics

The most important thing I hope to teach you about rotary cutting is to close your blade after cutting. I know from experience that an open blade can nick fabric in an unwanted place. Not only that, but having four kids taught me to keep that blade closed and out of sight!

Safety is important, but you don't need to be afraid of the rotary cutter. I'll take you through holding the ruler and cutter, straightening the fabric edge and cutting straight strips. Practice safe techniques from the start and you'll be fine. Oh, and don't look away while you are cutting!

Lefties, please accept my apology up front. I am a righty, and the directions and pictures reflect that. I know you are great at adjusting to our "right" world, and I thank you.

Holding the Ruler

1 Use your fingertips to put pressure on the ruler. Keep two fingers off the ruler and on the fabric you are cutting—this adds stability and reduces the possibility of the fabric or ruler shifting. The measurements on different brands of rulers may differ, so use one brand of ruler throughout an entire project to avoid any frustration.

2 Keep a sharp blade in your rotary cutter. If it doesn't glide like a hot knife through butter, it is dull. I like to cut through up to eight layers at a time, so a sharp blade is crucial for stress-free cutting.

3 Keep your thumb and fingers far enough from the ruler edge to avoid adding them to your quilt. The blade is very sharp!

Straightening the Fabric

1 To prepare fabric for cutting, grab the selvages (above left) and let the fabric hang down. Shift the edges until the fabric hangs flat with no ripples (above right).

2 When the fabric is hanging flat, gently place it on the cutting mat and bring the selvages to the folded edge. Do not pat or pull the fabric. Gently layer it to keep it straight and allow cutting through four layers at once.

Cutting the Straight Edge

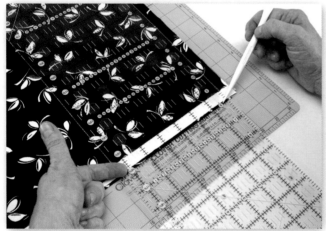

1 Straighten the edge by lining up a horizontal marking on the ruler with the bottom and top of the fabric and cut a clean edge.

2 Check to make sure all four layers are cut by pulling up the strip that was just cut off. It should be a continuous cross-grained strip. If it is in pieces, slide back the ruler and cut a new straight edge a bit farther back. Check the strip again. Spin the mat around to put the straight edge on the left to begin cutting strips.

Cutting Strips

1 Using the ruler measurements for cutting, line up the ruler marking on the cut fabric edge at the desired measurement. Then use the edge of the ruler as a guide for the rotary cutter. Quickly roll the cutter away from you, against the edge of the ruler, with steady downward pressure. Keep the rotary cutter perpendicular to the cutting surface for the most accurate cut.

2 To check if you are getting a straight cut, unfold a cut strip and let it hang down. If it has bends and turns in it like the fabric on the left, the fabric needs to be straightened and refolded. If the strip hangs straight and true, keep cutting!

I advise periodically checking strips as you are cutting to maintain straight, usable strips. Skipping this step may allow wavy and unusable strips to sneak in and add frustration to this otherwise delightful experience.

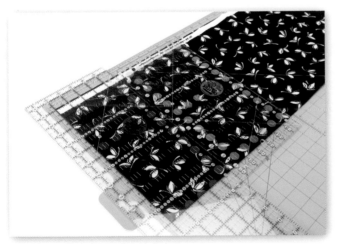

3 If you need to cut a very wide strip, you can use the mat markings or put two rulers together to get the correct width.

Design Basics

The Fibonacci Sequence

The Fibonacci sequence (0, 1, 1, 2, 3, 5, 8, 13, 21, 34, 55. . .) is a very useful set of numbers introduced by Fibonacci (a contraction of *filius Bonaccio*, "son of Bonaccio") in 1202. Unbeknownst to him, the sequence had actually been previously described in Indian mathematics.

The first two numbers of the sequence are 0 and 1, and each following number is the sum of the previous two: 0+1=1, 1+1=2, 1+2=3, and so on. The series is seen in nature and is used by artists, too.

The block at right demonstrates one example of how the Fibonacci sequence can be used in quilting. Here, the pieces spiral out, increasing in size according to the Fibonacci sequence; each square's measurements are based on the previous two. Because the sequence has acknowledged balance and visual interest, a set of block sizes is right there for your use. Not only can you utilize the actual sequence, you could also use the pattern but start on another number for different-sized blocks (for example: 2+2=4, 2+4=6, 4+6=10, 6+10=16, etc.).

Artistic Balance

Long ago, I learned that when matting artwork, the bottom should be larger than the top and sides. This artistic balance is easy to achieve with any size panel project. Simply use a larger border on the bottom of the quilt than on the top and sides.

The Golden Ratio

Another design building block is the golden ratio. Artists and architects have used the ratio to proportion their works since at least the Renaissance. The ratio is clearly evident, as seen in the golden rectangle. The ratio of the longer side of the rectangle to the shorter side uses the golden ratio to create the golden rectangle.

Appearing throughout nature, the ratio is easily seen in reference to the human body and as a gauge of beauty. Our arms, legs, fingers, teeth and faces, to mention a few, are all balanced according to the golden rectangle and ratio.

One can also see the ratio in objects such as flower heads, ram's horns, fish, snails, petals and stars.

Use the ratio as a foolproof design tool. Completely intertwined, the Fibonacci sequence and golden ratio are solid tools for design success. Look around—they are everywhere!

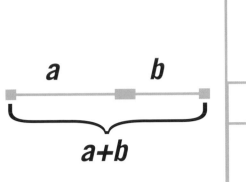

$a+b$ is to a as a is to b

The Golden Ratio

The Golden Rectangle

Using the Ratio for Your Designs
This preprinted panel can be cut out as a golden rectangle. Instant success!

SECTION 2
The Projects

Whittling down the project list for this book was very difficult. There are almost as many quilts that didn't make it in as those that did! The chosen quilts were created with simple design techniques that can be applied to similar-sized panels and large-scale prints.

This book's blueprint forced me to look at my stash a little differently and verbalize the design principles I use unconsciously so that I could share them with you. I had great fun pulling out old panels and finding terrific new fabrics, along with some of the newest panels and creatively printed yard goods. If I have done my work, you will wind up with a loaded design tool belt and the inspiration to plug your stashed-away panels into the models I've provided. You will look at the currently available panels in a new way and will be able to use your tool belt to draft your own quilts!

Panel Panache (page 30) and *Greet the Day* (page 102) provide directions to easily pop in one of today's widely available batik panels. *Fractured Flowers* (page 74) uses a contemporary large floral that can easily be substituted. Adjust the colors and away you go! Another project that can support simple substitution is

Gentle Morning (page 96). Not only can any toile be used, but any print with a dynamite motif could be set into the modified log cabin blocks. Photographic panels could be used to create memory quilts.

Embrace your memories by digging in your stash for pillow panels to embellish *Wandering Walrus* (page 48) and *Annie Gets Quilted* (page 38). It is so fun to go green and use up some of those hidden gems while learning the technique of broderie perse. Old standards are never out of style!

There are some amazing new fabrics available that utilize innovative printing. Lengthwise stripes, checkerboard blocks, and all of the current panels are simple to use and allow quilters to work faster and smarter. *Stripe It Stunning* (page 88), *Wise Words* (page 56), *Wise Water* (page 66) and *SewPlay* (page 108) are all created with the very newest fabric offerings. New large-scale floral batiks are used in *Inchworm* (page 82). These designs are certainly not limited to the fabrics they are shown in, so have fun shopping! You may find some of the fabrics still available, but dig around and you may find some that you like even better. Most of all, enjoy the quilts and get sewing!

Panel Panache
31" × 28½"
Pieced and quilted by the author
Fabrics courtesy of Island Batiks, Inc.

This little quilt is so fun to make! To come up with this design, I started with a dynamite batik panel by Island Batiks, Inc. A few simple numbers provided the tools to create this interesting and dynamic quilt. Learn more about the principles used in this design on page 32.

My Fabric Selections

FABRIC REQUIREMENTS

Batik Panel: at least 18" × 18"

Red Batik: ¼ yd.

Gold Batik: ¼ yd.

Striped Black Batik (piecing and binding): ⅞ yd.

Circle Print Black Batik: ⅓ yd.

Tree Print Black Batik: ⅓ yd.

Solid Black Batik: ⅓ yd.

Backing: 1 yd.

Batting: 39" × 36½"

CUTTING INSTRUCTIONS

BATIK PANEL:
Trim to 17" wide × 18" tall

RED BATIK:
Cut 1 strip 5½"

GOLD BATIK:
Cut 1 strip 5½"

STRIPED BLACK BATIK:
Cut 1 strip 5½"
Cut 1 strip 4"; from this strip:
    Cut 1 strip 4" × 18"
Cut 1 square 18" for 2¼" continuous bias binding

CIRCLE PRINT BLACK BATIK:
Cut 1 strip 5½"
Cut 1 strip 4"; from this strip:
    Cut 1 strip 4" × 11"

TREE PRINT BLACK BATIK:
Cut 1 strip 5½"
Cut 1 strip 4"; from this strip:
    Cut 1 strip 4" × 7½"

SOLID BLACK BATIK:
Cut 2 strips 4"; from these strips:
    Cut 1 strip 4" × 17"
    Cut 1 strip 4" × 28½"

Batik Panel for the Quilt Center

NOTES ON THIS QUILT

Once I had selected my panel, I designed the rest of the quilt around it. Using different-sized strips of black batik, I eyeballed the size that adequately framed the panel without looking too skinny or too fat. I did not use any mathematical formula; I just went with my gut. Working backward to come up with a formula to use again later, I can divide the finished measurement of the border by the panel measurement. The border finishes at 3½" and the height of the panel is 17½". If I divide the height by the border, it is a ratio of 5:1. That ratio will be a helpful starting point when determining a border width for other projects as well: Put that tool in your design belt!

Because the border will finish at 3½", I used that same measurement for my block sizes in the left border. Things look better in groups of three (at least to those of us who are not fond of symmetry), so I created three rows of blocks for the left border. Staggering the blocks also adds interest.

The bottom border is also based on 3½". Its height is 7" (the equivalent of two blocks). This added size on the bottom of the piece anchors it and adds weight. Sure, you could continue the 3½" black border all around the panel, but you will miss the fabric shopping, the piecing fun and this dynamic end result!

The Black Border Strips

A Left Border Block

The Bottom Border

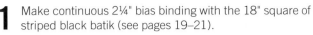

PREPARATION

1 Make continuous 2¼" bias binding with the 18" square of striped black batik (see pages 19–21).

2 Put a new blade in your rotary cutter. You will appreciate the accuracy and speed it provides.

3 Locate the 5½" strips of red and gold batik. Cut a 5½" × 22" piece of each. Set aside the remaining portion of each color for later piecing.

4 Locate the three black print 5½" strips. Cut a 5½" × 22" piece of each. Set aside the remaining portion of each for later piecing.

SUBCUTTING THE HOURGLASS BLOCKS

1 Layer one black print 5½" × 22" strip right sides together with the red 5½" × 22" strip.

2 Cut through both layers to make four 5½" squares. Do not move the squares.

3 Using the 45° line on your ruler, cut each square from corner to corner to make half-square triangles. Don't move the sets.

4 Using the 45° line on your ruler, cut each square from corner to corner again to make quarter-square triangles. Carefully move the sets, keeping the units together.

PREPARATION Step 4

SUBCUTTING THE HOURGLASS BLOCKS Step 1

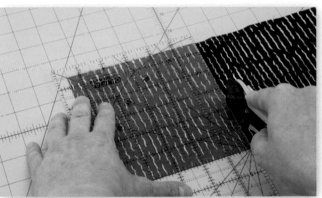

SUBCUTTING THE HOURGLASS BLOCKS Step 2

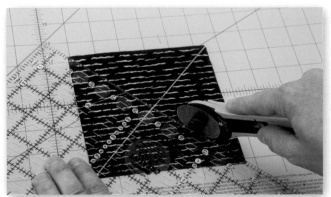

SUBCUTTING THE HOURGLASS BLOCKS Step 4

SUBCUTTING THE HOURGLASS BLOCKS Step 3

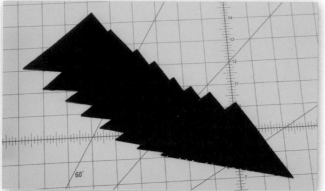

SUBCUTTING THE HOURGLASS BLOCKS Step 6

5 Repeat with a gold and black print set and a set with two different black prints. You will have two black strips left over. Set those aside for later piecing.

6 Neatly stack the triangle sets on your cutting mat. Place them with the red or gold pieces on top. The set with two different black prints will have a black piece on top.

7 Put the 90° corner of the triangles in the upper right-hand position. This step will greatly simplify your life. Please don't skip it!

8 Place the cutting mat, with the stacks resting beautifully on it, to the left of your sewing machine, within reaching distance while seated.

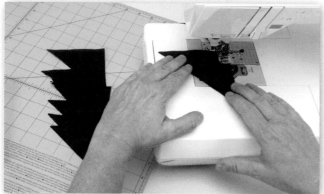

PIECING THE HOURGLASS BLOCKS Step 1

PIECING THE HOURGLASS BLOCKS

1 Yes! We finally get to sew! Pick up one triangle set (with the color on top) and sew from the 90° corner down to the point.

2 Chain sew all the triangle sets. Clip the threads between the sets and press the seam allowances to the black side.

3 Take two sets with different fabrics and put them right sides together, nestling the seam allowances.

4 Sew down the long edge, corner to corner. Handle them carefully since these are bias edges. Repeat for a total of twenty-four sets. Press the blocks open.

5 Square each hourglass block to 4".

PIECING THE HOURGLASS BLOCKS Step 2

PIECING THE HOURGLASS BLOCKS Step 3

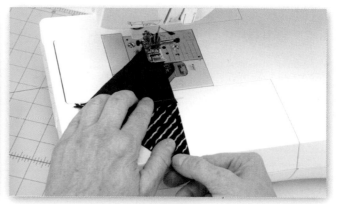

PIECING THE HOURGLASS BLOCKS Step 4

PLACING THE BLOCKS

1 On a design wall, place the hourglass blocks in three vertical rows. Row 1 has three blocks, Row 2 has five blocks and Row 3 has six blocks.

You will have extra hourglass blocks, so you can choose the blocks most pleasing to your eye. Notice how in the example at right the colors alternate position to almost make pinwheels.

When you are pleased with your block placement, sew each row together vertically.

2 Locate the three black print strips that were set aside for borders. Sew the 4" × 18½" border strip to the top of Row 1.

3 Sew the 4" × 11" border strip to the top of Row 2.

4 Sew the 4" × 7½" border strip to the top of Row 3.

5 Press the seams in Row 1 and Row 3 down. Press the seams in Row 2 up.

6 Sew the three rows together in order and press the seams to one side.

Row 1   Row 2   Row 3

PLACING THE BLOCKS Step 6

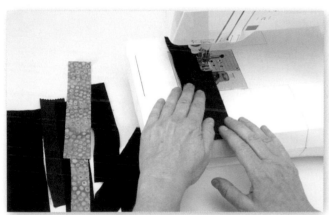

PIECING THE STRIPED UNIT Step 1

PIECING THE STRIPED UNIT

1 Gather the leftover red, gold and black strips that were set aside for later piecing. This is later piecing!

2 Cut an assortment of strips from the red, gold and black prints. Cut the strips in widths from 1½" × 8" to 2½" × 8".

3 Piece the strips together to make a unit that is approximately 8" × 18". Press all seams one way.

4 Square the unit to 7½" × 17".

PIECING THE STRIPED UNIT Step 3

ADDING THE BORDERS Step 1

ADDING THE BORDERS

1 Sew the 17" × 7½" striped unit to the bottom of the panel.

2 Sew the black 17" × 4" strip to the top of the panel. Press both seams up.

3 Sew the hourglass unit to the left side of the panel.

ADDING THE BORDERS Step 2

ADDING THE BORDERS Step 3

4 Sew the black 4" × 28½" strip to the right side of the panel unit.

5 Press both seams to the right, and you have a beautiful wall hanging ready to be layered and quilted.

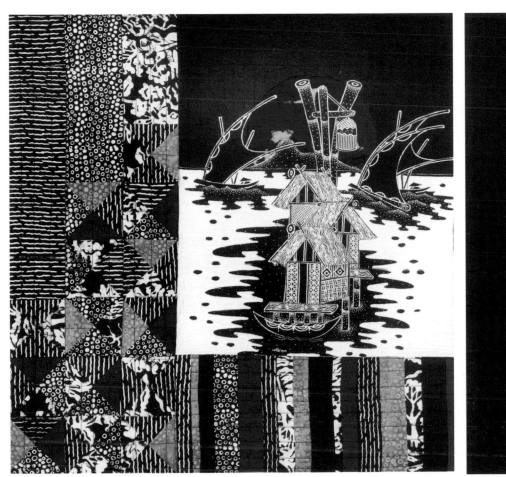

ADDING THE BORDERS Step 4

FINISHING THE QUILT

1 Layer, quilt and bind your one-of-a-kind work of art.

2 I quilted using stitch-in-the-ditch, straight parallel lines, diagonal serpentine stitches and zigzags to add textural interest to the piece. Adding the water quilting in the panel brings the liquid motif from the background to the foreground as an additional design element.

3 Binding is very important to my designs. As always, a decision had to be made about whether the quilt should have a definite ending or frame, or if the design should continue beyond its borders. No exclamation point or period here. This quilt is punctuated with gentle waves continuing to lap against the shore.

FINISHING THE QUILT Step 3

Annie Gets Quilted
52½" × 56½"
Pieced and quilted by the author
Fabrics (excluding panel) courtesy of
Marcus Fabrics

Preprinted pillow panels have been around for as long as I can remember. They're so cute and simple, I snatch them up to make easy homemade gifts. Do I actually make them, though? Apparently not, because I still have them hiding in my stash! This particularly adorable one—*Little Orphan Annie*—leaves pillow world behind to become the centerpiece of this bold and balanced quilt.

FABRIC REQUIREMENTS

Little Orphan Annie Panel (or similar graphic panel)

Large-Scale Black with White Polka Dots: ⅞ yd.

A Bit More Subdued Large-Scale Black with White Polka Dots: ⅓ yd.

Large-Scale Black with White Fronds: ½ yd.

Black-and-White Plaid: ¼ yd.

Black Tone-on-Tone: ¾ yd.

Black with White Small-Scale Polka Dots: ⅛ yd.

White with Small-Scale Polka Dots: ⅛ yd.

White with Black Herringbone: ½ yd.

White with Black Bacteria: ½ yd.

White with Large-Scale Black Leaves: ⅞ yd.

White with Large-Scale Black Clouds: ⅝ yd.

Orange with Red Floral: ⅛ yd.

Backing: 3½ yds.

Batting: 60½" × 64½"

Fusible Web: to fit Panel and muslin duplicate

White Muslin: to fit Panel

CUTTING INSTRUCTIONS

LARGE-SCALE BLACK WITH WHITE POLKA DOTS:
Cut 3 strips 8½"; from these strips:
   Cut 11 squares 8½"

A BIT MORE SUBDUED LARGE-SCALE BLACK WITH WHITE POLKA DOTS:
Cut 1 strip 8½"; from this strip:
   Cut 3 rectangles 8½" × 13½"

LARGE-SCALE BLACK WITH WHITE FRONDS:
Cut 2 strips 5½"; from these strips:
   Cut 11 squares 5½"

BLACK-AND-WHITE PLAID:
Cut 2 strips 3½"; from these strips:
   Cut 22 squares 3½"

BLACK TONE-ON-TONE:
Cut 1 strip 1½"; from this strip:
   Cut 1 strip 1½" × 20"
Cut 1 square 23" for 2¼" continuous bias binding

BLACK WITH WHITE SMALL-SCALE POLKA DOTS:
Cut 1 strip 2½"; from this strip:
   Cut 11 squares 2½"

WHITE WITH SMALL-SCALE POLKA DOTS:
Cut 1 strip 1½"; from this strip:
   Cut 1 strip 1½" × 20"

WHITE WITH BLACK HERRINGBONE:
Cut 2 strips 5½"; from these strips:
   Cut 11 squares 5½"

WHITE WITH BLACK BACTERIA:
Cut 1 strip 8½"; from this strip:
   Cut 1 rectangle 8½" × 13½"
Cut 1 strip 2½"; from this strip:
   Cut 11 squares 2½"

WHITE WITH LARGE-SCALE BLACK LEAVES:
Cut 3 strips 8½"; from these strips:
   Cut 2 rectangles 8½" × 13½"
   Cut 6 squares 8½"

WHITE WITH LARGE-SCALE BLACK CLOUDS:
Cut 2 strips 8½"; from these strips:
   Cut 5 squares 8½"

ORANGE WITH RED FLORAL:
Cut 1 strip 1½"; from this strip:
   Cut 2 strips 1½" × 20"

The *Little Orphan Annie* Panel

Using High-Contrast Fabrics for Emphasis

Finished Light Block

NOTES ON THIS QUILT

To utilize this panel in a larger way than a pillow, I appliquéd *Annie* to a pieced background. Cutting out portions of a print and placing them on a whole cloth background is always a sure way to create a stunning showpiece. In fact, the technique of using chintzy fabrics for appliqué has been used continually through the life of quilting. Long ago in England, quilters used fabrics imported from India, cutting out the trendy floral, oriental or Tree of Life motifs to appliqué to their projects. Not only were they stretching their purchase by using small portions of nice fabric, but they were also showing off their handwork skills.

Here, I've applied this technique with a much less intricate motif and contemporary fusing methods. Same idea, just much simpler!

With such a bold appliqué to support, this quilt needs clear-cut lines and sturdy, sizable blocks to support and accent the vivid *Annie*s. Sparked with off-center color, the blocks are based on the Fibonacci sequence (see page 26). The sizes of the block components are 1", 1", 2", 3", 5" and 8" squares. The finished block is an 8" × 13" rectangle. The block is structurally strong and solid, perfect to underline and support *Annie*.

Not only is the core design clear, but the fabric choices add to the clean, sharp look. The very large-scale prints, combined with the geometric medium-scale prints and simplistic small-scale pieces, add a "funny paper" simplicity with their measured steps in scale. A more homogenous mixture of scales would reduce the clarity and "larger than life" feel.

The high contrast of the Sunday cartoons is emphasized with vastly different scales and values in fabrics and is echoed with the highly contrasting black-and-white prints.

Finished Dark Block

5"			8"
3"	1"	1"	
	2"		

Fibonacci Sequence Block

PIECING THE DARK BLOCKS

1 Layer the 20" white with small-scale polka-dot strip with a 20" orange with red floral print strip and stitch together.

2 Set the seam toward the orange strip and press the strips open.

3 Move the strip set to the cutting mat and subcut eleven strips 1½" wide.

4 Move the subsets to the left side of the machine. Place 2½" squares of white with black bacteria fabric to the right of the subsets.

5 Layer the two pieces right sides together and stitch. Repeat for all eleven sections.

6 Set the seam toward the 2½" square and press open.

7 Place these sections to the left of the sewing machine with the orange square in the bottom right position. The 3½" squares of black-and-white plaid go directly to the right of the subsets.

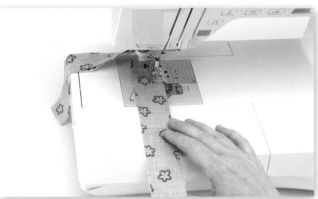

PIECING THE DARK BLOCKS Step 1

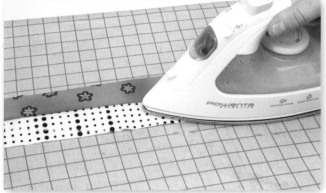

PIECING THE DARK BLOCKS Step 2

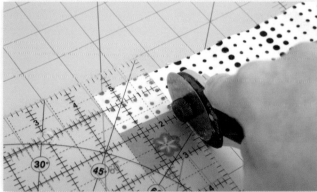

PIECING THE DARK BLOCKS Step 3

PIECING THE DARK BLOCKS Step 4

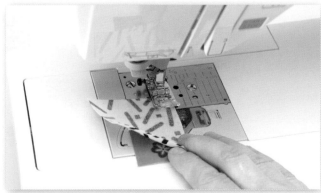

PIECING THE DARK BLOCKS Step 5

PIECING THE DARK BLOCKS Step 7

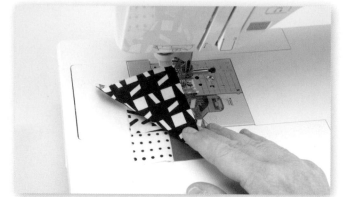

PIECING THE DARK BLOCKS Step 8

8 Layer and piece the units together, making sure the end with the orange square goes through the machine last. Repeat for all eleven blocks.

9 Set the seam toward the 3½" block and press open.

10 Continue making the block by placing the newly pieced units to the left of the machine with the orange square toward the lower right and the 5½" frond square on the right side.

11 Layer the pieces right sides together and stitch. Repeat for all eleven blocks.

12 Set the seam toward the 5½" square and press open.

13 Finish the dark blocks by placing the units to the left of the machine. The pieced section has the orange square near the bottom right and an 8½" square of large-scale black with white polka dots is to the right.

14 Layer the pieces and stitch. Repeat for all eleven blocks.

15 Set the seam toward the 8½" square and press open. The dark blocks are all done!

PIECING THE DARK BLOCKS Step 10

PIECING THE DARK BLOCKS Step 13

PIECING THE DARK BLOCKS Step 15

PIECING THE LIGHT BLOCKS

1 Layer the 20" black tone-on-tone strip right sides together with a 20" orange strip and stitch together.

2 Set the seam toward the orange strip and press the strips open.

3 Move the strip set to the cutting mat and subcut eleven strips 1½" wide.

4 Move the subsets to the left side of the machine. Place the 2½" black with white small-scale polka-dot squares to the right of the subsets.

5 Layer the two pieces right sides together and stitch. Repeat for all eleven sections.

6 Set the seam toward the 2½" square and press open.

7 Place the newly pieced sections to the left of the sewing machine with the orange square in the bottom right position. The 3½" black-and-white plaid square goes directly to the right.

8 Layer and piece the units together, making sure the end with the orange square goes through the machine last. Repeat for all eleven blocks.

PIECING THE LIGHT BLOCKS Step 4

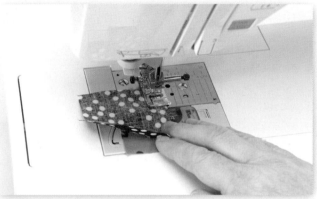

PIECING THE LIGHT BLOCKS Step 5

PIECING THE LIGHT BLOCKS Step 6

PIECING THE LIGHT BLOCKS Step 7

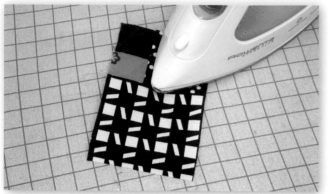

PIECING THE LIGHT BLOCKS Step 9

9 Set the seam toward the 3½" square and press open.

10 Continue making the block by placing the pieced units to the left of the machine, with the orange square on the lower right and the 5½" herringbone square on the right side.

11 Layer the pieces right sides together and stitch. Repeat for all eleven blocks.

12 Set the seam toward the 5½" square and press open.

13 Finish the light blocks by placing the units to the left of the machine. The pieced section has the orange square near the bottom right and the 8½" cloud print square directly on the right.

14 Layer the pieces and stitch. Repeat for all eleven blocks.

15 Set the seam toward the 8½" square and press open. Now the light blocks are all done.

PIECING THE LIGHT BLOCKS Step 10

PIECING THE LIGHT BLOCKS Step 13

PIECING THE LIGHT BLOCKS Step 15

APPLIQUÉING *ANNIE*

1 Stitch the white with black bacteria print 8½" × 13½" rectangle to the black polka-dot print 8½" × 13½" rectangle along the long edge.

2 Add a white with black leaves 8½" × 13½" rectangle to the other side of the black polka-dot 8½" × 13½" rectangle.

3 Press the seams toward the dark rectangle. This is the appliqué background for the front of *Annie*.

4 Stitch a black polka-dot print 8½" × 13½" rectangle to each side of a white with black leaves 8½" × 13½" rectangle and press the seams toward the dark rectangles. This is the appliqué background for the back of *Annie*.

5 Layer the fusible web, with the sticky side down, on to the *Annie* appliqué. Put the appliqué right-side down so she is oriented the correct way to add the fusible web. Trim down the appliqué and fusible web around the applique, leaving a generous margin.

6 Checking that the sticky side is on the back of the appliqué, lightly fuse according to the manufacturer's recommendations.

7 Using the fused appliqué as a pattern, cut out an additional layer of fusible web and white muslin. Adding a layer of white muslin behind the thin appliqué will help keep the color bright. The black-and-white piecing would show through without this extra layer.

8 Lightly fuse the web to the white muslin and then peel the paper off the *Annie* appliqué.

9 Layer *Annie* with the white muslin appliqué and lightly fuse together.

APPLIQUÉING *ANNIE* Step 5

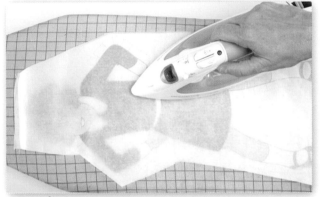
APPLIQUÉING *ANNIE* Step 6

APPLIQUÉING *ANNIE* Step 7

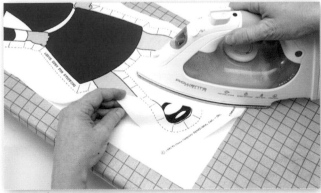
APPLIQUÉING *ANNIE* Step 9

APPLIQUÉING *ANNIE* Step 8

10 Remove the paper from the white muslin and carefully cut out around the appliqué.

11 Repeat this process for the back of *Annie* and the text bubble.

12 Fuse the front of *Annie* to the white/black/white appliqué background.

13 Fuse the back of *Annie* and the text bubble to the black/white/black appliqué background.

14 Using black thread to define the appliqué, machine appliqué around the edges of both the front and back of *Annie* with a satin stitch.

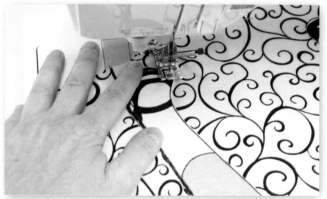

APPLIQUÉING *ANNIE* Step 10

APPLIQUÉING *ANNIE* Step 14

MAKING THE VERTICAL ROWS

1 Lay out four dark blocks with the orange square in the upper right position, alternating with three light blocks with the orange square in the lower left position.

2 Stitch the blocks together and press the seams toward the dark blocks. This is Row 1.

3 Lay out four light blocks with the orange square in the upper right position, alternating with three dark blocks with the orange square in the lower left position.

4 Stitch the blocks together and press the seams toward the dark blocks. This is Row 4.

5 Row 2 starts with a light block—with the orange square in the upper right position above a dark block with the orange square in the bottom left position. Stitch those two blocks together. Add another light block, with the orange square in the upper right position, and press the seams toward the dark block.

6 Sew a light block, with the orange square in the upper right position to the bottom of the back of *Annie* appliqué section. Press the seam toward the dark block.

7 Join the two partial rows to make Row 2 and press the seam toward the dark block.

8 Sew a dark block, with the orange in the upper right position, to the top of the front of the *Annie* appliqué section. Press the seam toward the dark block.

VERTICAL ROWS Step 2

VERTICAL ROWS Step 4

9 Make a three-block partial row with two dark blocks, with the orange square in the upper right position, sandwiching a light block with the orange square in the bottom left position.

10 Add the three-block partial row to the bottom of the front of *Annie* appliqué and press all seams toward the dark blocks. This is Row 3.

VERTICAL ROWS Step 7

VERTICAL ROWS Step 10

FINISHING THE QUILT

1 Lay out the rows in order and sew Row 1 to Row 2, nestling seams together for clean corners.

2 Sew Row 3 to Row 4, making sure the seams are nestled together.

3 Join the two units to make the complete quilt top and press the seams all one way.

4 Layer, quilt and bind your masterpiece!

Row 1   Row 2   Row 3   Row 4

FINISHING QUILT Step 4

Wandering Walrus
48" × 63½"
Pieced and quilted by the author

This chubby little walrus started out his life as a pillow panel, but I found a home for him on this quilt, appliquéd over a backdrop of blocks reminiscent of the traditional courthouse steps block. For even more whimsy, the back side of the walrus can be added to the quilt back. This is a fun element to add to a baby quilt! If the front of the quilt gets dirty, just flip it over, and the walrus is still there.

FABRIC REQUIREMENTS

Walrus Panel, Hallmark 1980 (or similar graphic panel)

Red/Pink Small-Scale Check: ⅜ yd.

Black Tone-on-Tone with Circles: ¼ yd.

Medium Dark Black with White Medium-Scale Print: ⅝ yd.

Medium White with Black Lace Large-Scale Print: ⅝ yd.

Medium Light White with Black Small-Scale Print: ⅞ yd.

Black-and-White Large Check: 1¾ yds.

Black Tone-on-Tone Binding: ¾ yd.

Flannel Backing: 3¼ yds.

Batting: 56" × 71½"

Fusible Web: to fit Panel pieces

CUTTING INSTRUCTIONS

RED/PINK SMALL-SCALE CHECK:
Cut 1 strip 3"
Cut 3 strips 2½"

BLACK TONE-ON-TONE WITH CIRCLES:
Cut 2 strips 3"

MEDIUM DARK BLACK WITH WHITE MEDIUM-SCALE PRINT:
Cut 5 strips 3"; from these strips:
    Cut 24 strips 3" × 8"

MEDIUM WHITE WITH BLACK LACE LARGE-SCALE PRINT:
Cut 5 strips 3"; from these strips:
    Cut 24 strips 3" × 8"

MEDIUM LIGHT WHITE WITH BLACK SMALL-SCALE PRINT:
Cut 8 strips 3"; from these strips:
    Cut 24 strips 3" × 13"

BLACK-AND-WHITE LARGE CHECK:
Cut 1 strip 5½" × 52½" (lengthwise to avoid piecing)
Cut 1 strip 8½" × 45" (lengthwise to avoid piecing)
Cut 1 strip 3½" × 60½" (lengthwise to avoid piecing)
Cut 1 strip 3½" × 48" (lengthwise to avoid piecing)

BLACK TONE-ON-TONE BINDING:
Cut 1 square 24" for 2¼" continuous bias binding

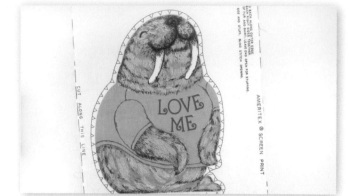

The Walrus Panel

Measuring the Block

A Variation on the Traditional Courthouse Steps Block

Placing the Back Side of the Panel on the Back of the Quilt

Adding Stitching to the Appliqué

NOTES ON THIS QUILT

Though I wanted this adorable walrus to be a focal point of the quilt, I didn't want it to dominate the piece. As such, I built a large block reminiscent of a traditional courthouse steps block to provide a solid base to support the walrus. To prevent the blocks from overpowering the panel, I measured the walrus and decided that the blocks should be no more than two-thirds the size of the walrus—this way the block enhances the panel.

Much as a log cabin block does, the traditional courthouse steps block starts with a center block and adds strips around the center. The strips are added from side to side and then top and bottom instead of going around the center. In this quilt, I varied the traditional design by starting with a large square in the center and built the strips outward, with the darkest value on the first logs, lightening the strips with each set. This variation contradicts the traditional value placement that maintains similar values on each side of the block to create a pyramid effect. It also allows the outer logs to blend when the block orientation is alternated in the layout.

The walrus is appliquéd using fusible web with stitching all the way around the perimeter. I don't typically add this step with fusible appliqué, but this is a baby quilt, and I wanted it to be washable and durable. Stitching the edges with bold red thread adds protection and outlines the appliqué beautifully; using decorative stitching within the appliqué creates additional interest and texture in this contemporary *broderie perse*.

BUILDING THE BLOCKS

1 Create a strip set by layering a 3" red/pink checked strip on to a 3" black strip with circles, right sides together, and then sewing them together.

2 Add a 3" black strip to the other side of the red/pink checked strip and press all of the seams out toward the black strips.

3 Move the strip set to the cutting mat and subcut twelve segments 3" wide.

4 Stitch a 3" × 8" medium dark black with white medium-scale print strip to one side of the 3" pieced segment.

5 Sandwich the 3" pieced segment with another 3" × 8" medium dark black with white medium-scale print strip by adding it to the other side of the segment; press the seams out.

6 Rotate the block 90° and stitch a 3" × 8" medium white with black lace large-scale print on each end of the block. Press the seams out.

7 Rotate the block another 90° and add a 3" × 13" medium light white with black small-scale print strip to one side of the block. Complete the block with a final 3" × 13" strip on the opposite side and press the seams out. Repeat for all twelve blocks.

Using Fabric to Add Visual Interest

I once heard that any quilt block over the size of 8" finished had better be very interesting. Well, this block is much larger, and while the design is simple, the fabric choices create volumes of interest. The value shifts, along with the style and scale changes, make this block dynamic.

BUILDING THE BLOCKS Step 1

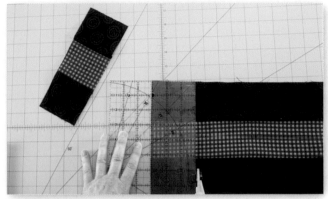

BUILDING THE BLOCKS Step 3

BUILDING THE BLOCKS Step 4

BUILDING THE BLOCKS Step 7

BUILDING THE BLOCKS Step 6

BUILDING THE QUILT CENTER Step 1

BUILDING THE QUILT CENTER

1 Create a partial row by putting two blocks together, alternating the rotation of the blocks. The block on the left will appear to be horizontal, and the block on the right will appear to be vertical. Stitch four sets of partial rows; press the seams toward the vertical blocks.

2 The quilt layout is four rows of three blocks each, so these partial rows zigzag row by row. On a design wall, place the partial rows, starting with a horizontal block in the top left.

3 Add a block in the horizontal position to the end of Row 1 and Row 3. Rows 2 and 4 get a vertical block in the beginning position.

4 Stitch the added blocks to their rows and press the seams toward the vertical blocks.

5 Join the four rows and press the seams down to complete the quilt center.

Row 1

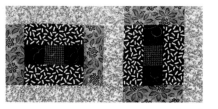

Row 2

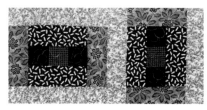

Row 3

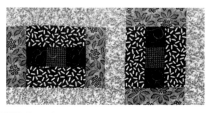

BUILDING THE QUILT CENTER Step 2   **Row 4**

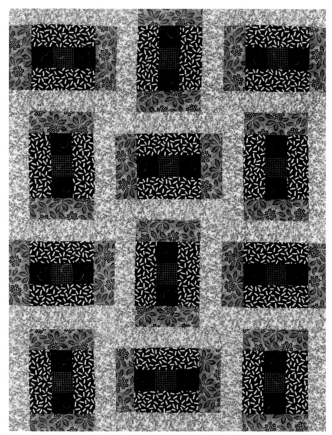

BUILDING THE QUILT CENTER Step 5

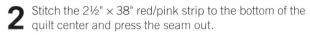

ADDING THE INNER BORDER

1 Cut a 2½" red/pink strip to 2½" × 38".

2 Stitch the 2½" × 38" red/pink strip to the bottom of the quilt center and press the seam out.

3 Cut one end of each remaining red/pink 2½" strip at a 90° angle, as shown top right with black fabric. Layer the ends and stitch a seam to join them, as shown mid-right with black fabric. Press the seam open. Cut the strip to 2½" × 52½".

4 Stitch the 2½" × 52½" red/pink border strip to the left side of the quilt center and press the seam out.

ADDING THE INNER BORDER Step 3

ADDING THE OUTER BORDER

1 Add the 5½" × 52½" black-and-white checked border strip to the left side of the quilt center and press the seam out.

2 Add the 8½" × 45" black-and-white checked border strip to the bottom of the quilt and press the seam out.

3 Add the 3½" × 60½" black-and-white checked border strip to the right side of the quilt and press the seam out.

4 Add the 3½" × 48" black-and-white checked border strip to the top of the quilt and press the seam out.

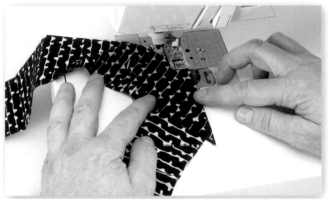

ADDING THE INNER BORDER Step 3

Framing Your Work with Asymmetrical Borders

The borders of this quilt are asymmetrical. I thank Mrs. Asp, my elementary and high school art teacher, for teaching me that when matting artwork, the bottom of the mat is wider than the top and sides. This knowledge has influenced my designs tremendously. In this quilt we see that the bottom border is wider and heavier than the side and top borders. This gives a weight and "right-side up" feel to this baby quilt. It also provides a solid surface for the walrus to rest on.

ADDING THE OUTER BORDER Steps 1, 2, 3 and 4

ADDING THE APPLIQUÉ Step 2

ADDING THE APPLIQUÉ Step 3

ADDING THE APPLIQUÉ Step 4

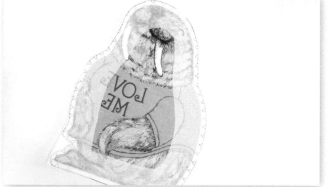

ADDING THE APPLIQUÉ Step 5

ADDING THE APPLIQUÉ Step 6

ADDING THE APPLIQUÉ Step 7

ADDING THE APPLIQUÉ

1 Cut out the walrus appliqués, leaving ¼" around the outside edges.

2 On the paper backing of fusible web, trace around the wrong side of the appliqué shapes.

3 Cut out the fusible web just outside the traced line.

4 Cut out the center of the fusible web about 2" inside the traced line. Removing the center will reduce bulk and stiffness from this large appliqué. If left intact, the appliqué could become stiff and not at all snuggly.

5 Lightly press the fusible web to the wrong side of the appliqué.

6 Cut out the walrus on the outer line of the appliqué.

7 Using the quilt photograph below for placement, fuse the appliqué to the quilt top. Also line up the back side of the walrus on the quilt back, and fuse. When you are positioning the back appliqué, remember that the quilt back has 4" extending from all sides of the quilt top.

8 Satin-stitch on all edges of the appliqués. Because the outline on the panel is a bit orange instead of red, I used a vivid red rayon thread that added a bit of sheen, a bit of color and a lot of texture to stitch over the outlines and writing on the appliqué.

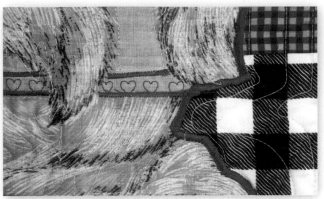

ADDING THE APPLIQUÉ Step 8

FINISHING THE QUILT

1 Layer the backing, batting and quilt top, lining up the front walrus appliqué and the back walrus appliqué. Use flower head pins to identify corners or significant spots in the appliqué through all three layers.

When the appliqués are lined up, pin the quilt layers together to secure them.

2 Quilt the three layers to enhance the appliqué. I echo quilted around the walrus to define him and then used straight lines and grids to complete the quilt top.

Additional quilting within the appliqué really allows the walrus to come to life.

FINISHING THE QUILT Step 1

FINISHING THE QUILT Step 2

wise words

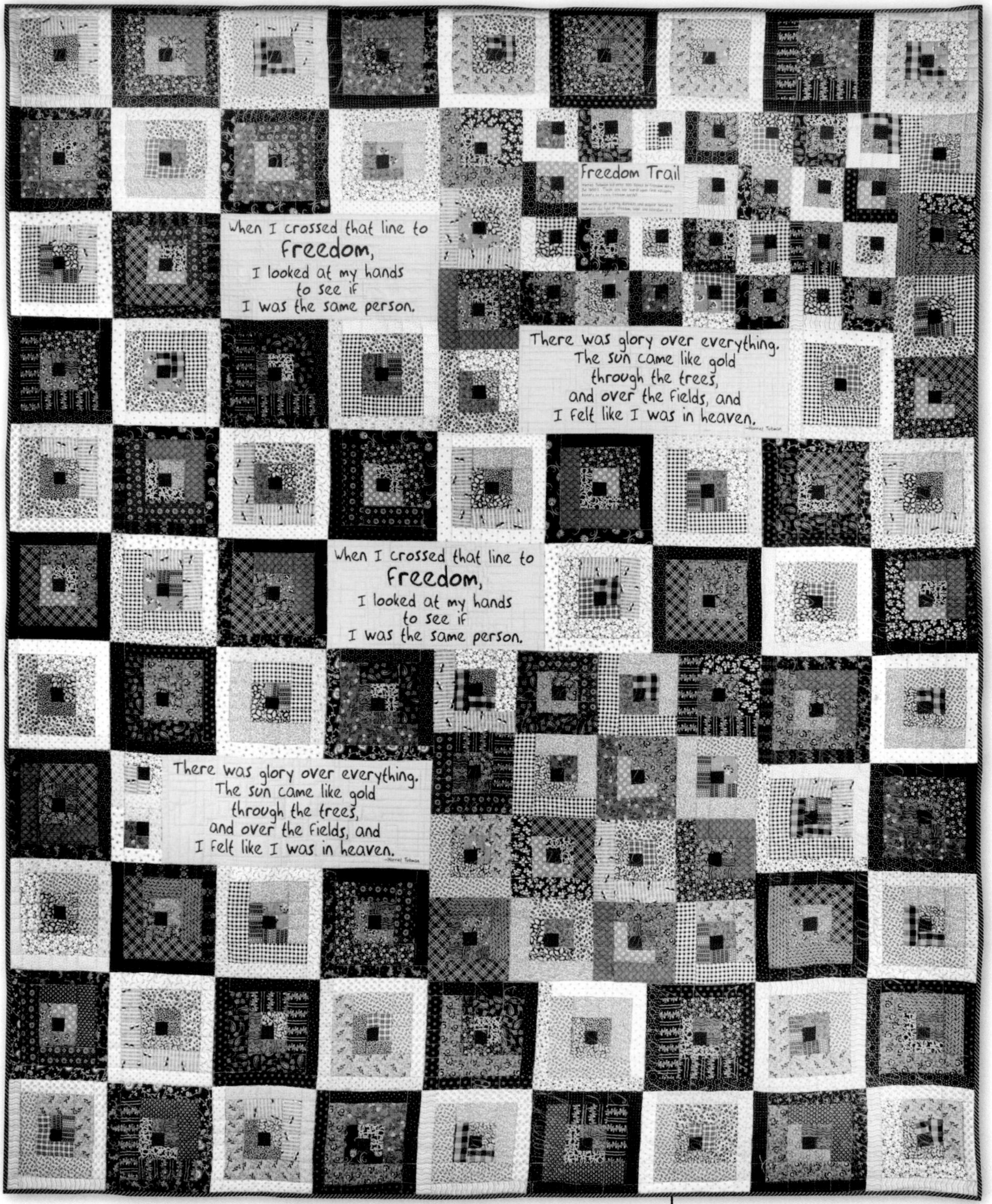
Freedom Trail
When I crossed that line to
Freedom,
I looked at my hands
to see if
I was the same person.
There was glory over everything.
The sun came like gold
through the trees,
and over the fields, and
I felt like I was in heaven.
When I crossed that line to
Freedom,
I looked at my hands
to see if
I was the same person.
There was glory over everything.
The sun came like gold
through the trees,
and over the fields, and
I felt like I was in heaven.

Wise Words
72½" × 88½"
Pieced and quilted by the author

This simple design, grounded in tradition, can provide a framework for printed panels, important family memories or dates, appliqué or any other art you choose to insert in the panel spaces. Highly flexible and adaptable, this design lends itself to many types of written words and other art. With Harriet Tubman's quotes embedded in log cabin blocks, it celebrates strength, beauty, tenacity and the fight for liberty. This quilt possessed an amazing energy while it took shape and retains that energy for me still.

Fabric Selection

Choose a variety of each type of fabric; I suggest at least five different Rusty Reds, Medium Lights and Medium Darks. These fabrics are used for the centers of the blocks; a variety of different centers creates more visual interest in the quilt.

FABRIC REQUIREMENTS

Quote Panels

Rusty Reds: ⅛ yd. each of 5 different fabrics

Lightest Light: 1⅝ yds. total

Light: 1½ yds. total

Medium Light: ⅞ yd. total

Medium Dark: ¾ yd. total

Dark: 1½ yds. total

Darkest Dark: 1⅝ yds. total

Binding: ⅞ yd.

Backing: 5¾ yds.

Batting: 80½" × 96½"

CUTTING INSTRUCTIONS

RUSTY REDS:
Cut 5 strips 1½" (one from each fabric); from these strips:
    Cut 10 strips 21" × 1½"

LIGHTEST LIGHT:
Cut 37 strips 1½"; from these strips:
    Cut 35 strips 1½" × 6½"
    Cut 70 strips 1½" × 7½"
    Cut 35 strips 1½" × 8½"
    Cut 15 strips 1½" × 2½"
    Cut 30 strips 1½" × 3½"
    Cut 15 strips 1½" × 4½"

LIGHT:
Cut 24 strips 2"; from these strips:
    Cut 47 strips 2" × 3½"
    Cut 94 strips 2" × 5"
    Cut 47 strips 2" × 6½"

MEDIUM LIGHT:
Cut 18 strips 1½"; from these strips:
    Cut 5 strips 1½" × 21" (one each from different fabrics)
    Cut 62 squares 1½"
    Cut 124 strips 1½" × 2½"
    Cut 62 strips 1½" × 3½"

MEDIUM DARK:
Cut 15 strips 1½"; from these strips:
    Cut 5 strips 1½" × 21" (one each from different fabrics)
    Cut 118 strips 1½" × 2½"
    Cut 59 strips 1½" × 3½"

DARK:
Cut 24 strips 2"; from these strips:
    Cut 46 strips 2" × 3½"
    Cut 92 strips 2" × 5"
    Cut 46 strips 2" × 6½"

DARKEST DARK:
Cut 35 strips 1½"; from these strips:
    Cut 34 strips 1½" × 6½"
    Cut 68 strips 1½" × 7½"
    Cut 34 strips 1½" × 8½"
    Cut 13 strips 1½" × 2½"
    Cut 26 strips 1½" × 3½"
    Cut 13 strips 1½" × 4½"

BINDING
Cut 1 square 29" for 2¼" continuous bias binding

> There was glory over everything.
> The sun came like gold
> through the trees,
> and over the fields, and
> I felt like I was in heaven.
>
> —Harriet Tubman

> When I crossed that line to
> **Freedom,**
> I looked at my hands
> to see if
> I was the same person.

Preprinted Panels

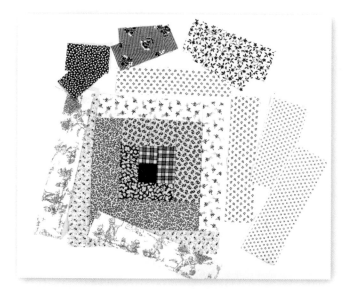

Fabric and Color

NOTES ON THIS QUILT

Inspiration

Wise Words is a tribute not only to the speaker, Harriet Tubman, but also to strong women everywhere. It is believed that Tubman said she could have freed more slaves if those folks had realized they were slaves. Sometimes our ignorance or refusal to open our mind keeps us from creative freedom as well. This quilt came into being because I was convinced to make a project with the dark and murky reproduction fabrics my friend Carrie loves. She insisted I get out of my box, branch out and try something new. In response to her, this piece was created to celebrate the willingness to take an uncertain step, whether great or small.

As I was making the quilt I had an overwhelming sense of empowerment. The history of the block and Harriet Tubman's story are very strong images for me.

Fabric and Color

I based the blocks in this quilt on the traditional log cabin block, which starts with a center square with "logs" placed around it in contrasting values. The opposite sides are generally light across from dark and of equal width. The contrasting sides provide the diagonal line that is an integral element of a log cabin block.

My adaptation of the log cabin block began with a traditional red square surrounded by 1" logs. The next layer of logs is wider and creates space within the block. The final log round returns to 1".

Along with the unequal log size, value placement in the block is also altered in my version. I wanted to emphasize the individual strength of each block, correlating to the individual strength of each passenger on the Underground Railroad.

Fabric selection for this quilt is fun! Block A uses all lights, separated into three graduated piles. The darkest lights will be placed around the center, and medium lights are the wider logs encircled by the lightest logs. Block B moves in the opposite value direction. The lightest darks encircle the center and graduate out to the darkest values in the outer ring.

Block Dimensions

My first step in designing this piece was to find a common denominator between the three different-sized quotation panels. The largest panels would easily finish at 8" × 20". The smallest panel could finish at 4" × 8", and the middle panel finishes at 8" × 16". A common denominator in all three blocks is 2". With that measurement, I could use 8" blocks as my starting point. Additional 6" and 4" blocks mesh with the 8" blocks to complete the design.

Because of the unequal log measurements, the outer ring can be omitted to create the 6" block, simplifying the quilt's construction.

Finding the Common Denominator for the Blocks
With a common deniminator of 2", the height of three 8" blocks will match four 6" blocks.
Likewise, 4" blocks will easily combine with the basic 8" block.

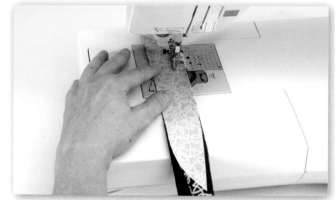

CONSTRUCTING THE LIGHT BLOCKS **Step 1**

CONSTRUCTING THE LIGHT BLOCKS **Step 3**

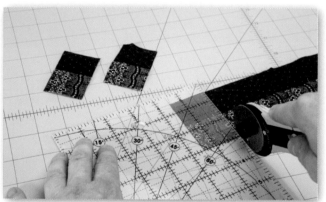

CONSTRUCTING THE LIGHT BLOCKS **Step 4**

CONSTRUCTING THE LIGHT BLOCKS

Finished 8" and 6" Blocks

Note: Throughout this pattern, the blocks will be referred to by their finished size, not by their cut size.

1 Layer a 21" × 1½" medium light strip, right sides together, with a 21" × 1½" red strip and stitch together.

2 Piece the four remaining medium light strips with four of the red strips.

3 Press the seam allowances of each set toward the medium light strips.

4 Cut the strip sets into sixty-two segments 1½" wide.

5 Move the segments to the left of the sewing machine along with the 2½" strips of the matching medium light fabric.

6 Add a 1½" × 2½" medium light strip and stitch. Always put on the bottom the piece that has already been sewn and layer the new strip on top. Also make sure the strip that was just added is fed through the machine first. This guarantees the logs will go around the center the same way every time. Repeat for all sixty-two light blocks.

7 Press the seams out toward the medium light strips.

8 Set aside fifteen of these units to be used later for the 4" light blocks (see page 62).

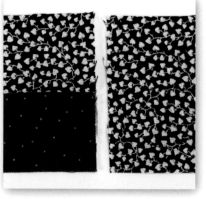

CONSTRUCTING THE LIGHT BLOCKS **Step 5**

CONSTRUCTING THE LIGHT BLOCKS **Step 7**

9 Using a different medium light fabric, add a 2½" medium light log to each remaining block, followed by a 3½" medium light log of the same fabric. Press the seams out.

10 Next, add a 2" × 3½" light log, remembering to put the previously sewn log into the machine first with the new log on top. Add a 2" × 5" light log of the same fabric and press the seams out.

11 Choose 5" and 6½" logs of another light fabric and add them to finish the ring. Press the seams out.

12 Repeat Steps 9–11 for each block. Set aside twelve of these units; these are the completed 6" light blocks.

13 Complete the 8" blocks by adding the final ring of logs. Sew a 6½" log of the lightest light fabric to the block, followed by a 7½" log of the same fabric.

14 Choose a different lightest light fabric for the 7½" and 8½" logs, add to the block and press the seams out.

15 Repeat Steps 13 and 14 for thirty-five light 8" blocks.

CONSTRUCTING THE LIGHT BLOCKS **Step 9**

CONSTRUCTING THE LIGHT BLOCKS **Step 10**

CONSTRUCTING THE LIGHT BLOCKS **Step 10**

CONSTRUCTING THE LIGHT BLOCKS **Step 11**

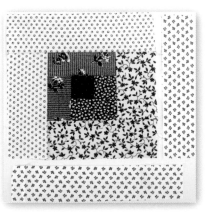

CONSTRUCTING THE LIGHT BLOCKS **Step 13**

CONSTRUCTING THE LIGHT BLOCKS **Step 14**

FINISHED 4" BLOCKS **Step 3**

FINISHED 4" BLOCKS **Step 4**

CONSTRUCTING THE DARK BLOCKS **Step 4**

CONSTRUCTING THE DARK BLOCKS **Step 7**

Finished 4" Blocks

1 Light 4" blocks are built with the center, first ring and an adapted second ring. To add contrast to the finished quilt top, the lightest fabrics are used for the second ring of the 4" blocks.

2 Retrieve the fifteen blocks set aside for the 4" blocks.

3 Sew a 1½" × 2½" lightest light log to the block, followed by a 1½" × 3½" lightest light log of the same fabric.

4 Finish the block with a 1½" × 3½" very lightest light log and a 1½" × 4½" very lightest light log of the same fabric and press the seams out.

5 Repeat Steps 1–4 for a total of fifteen light 4" blocks.

CONSTRUCTING THE DARK BLOCKS

Finished 8" and 6" Blocks

1 Layer a 1½" medium dark strip, right sides together, with a 1½" red strip and stitch together.

2 Piece the four remaining medium dark strips with the remaining red strips. Press the seam allowances toward the medium dark strips.

3 Cut the strip sets into fifty-nine segments 1½" wide. Move the segments to the left of the sewing machine along with the 2½" strips of the matching medium dark fabric.

4 Add a 1½" × 2½" medium dark strip and stitch. Always put on the bottom the piece that has already been sewn and layer the new strip on top. Also make sure the strip that was just added is fed through the machine first. This guarantees the logs will go around the center the same way every time. Stitch all fifty-nine units.

5 Press the seams out toward the medium dark strip.

6 Set aside thirteen of these units to be used later for the 4" dark blocks (see page 63).

7 Using a different medium dark fabric, add a 2½" medium dark log to each block, followed by a 3½" medium dark log of the same fabric. Press the seams out.

8 Next, add a 2" × 3½" dark log, remembering to put the previously sewn log into the machine first with the new log on top. Add a 2" × 5" dark log of the same fabric and press the seams out.

9 Choose 5" and 6½" logs of another dark fabric and add them to finish the ring. Press the seams out.

10 Repeat Steps 7–9 for each block. Set aside twelve of these units; these are the completed 6" light blocks.

11 Complete the 8" blocks by adding the final ring of darkest dark logs, making sure that the 6½" and 7½" logs are the same fabric. Choose a different fabric for the 7½" and 8½" logs, add them to the block and press the seams out.

12 Repeat Step 11 for all thirty-four dark 8" blocks.

Finished 4" Blocks

1 Dark 4" blocks are built with the center, first ring and an adapted second ring. To add contrast to the finished quilt top, the darkest fabrics are used for the second ring of the 4" dark blocks.

2 Retrieve the thirteen blocks set aside for dark 4" blocks.

3 Sew a 1½" × 2½" darkest dark log to the block, followed by a 1½" × 3½" darkest dark log of the same fabric.

4 Finish the block with a 1½" × 3½" darkest dark log of a different fabric and a 1½" × 4½" darkest dark log of the same fabric and press the seams out.

5 Repeat for a total of thirteen dark 4" blocks.

CONSTRUCTING THE DARK BLOCKS **Step 9**

CONSTRUCTING THE DARK BLOCKS **Step 11**

FINISHED 4" BLOCKS **Step 3**

FINISHED 4" BLOCKS **Step 4**

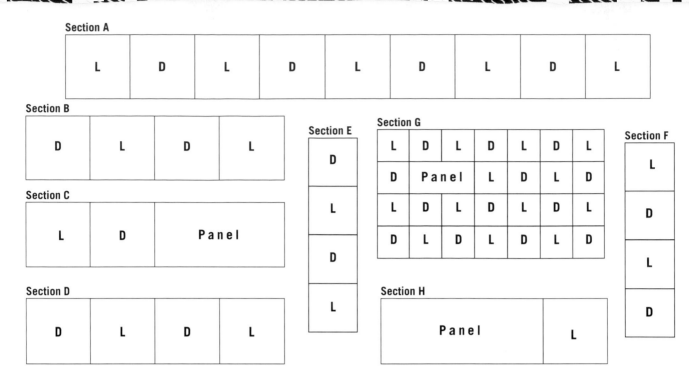

Section A

| L | D | L | D | L | D | L | D | L |

Section B

| D | L | D | L |

Section C

| L | D | Panel |

Section D

| D | L | D | L |

Section E

| D |
| L |
| D |
| L |

Section G

L	D	L	D	L	D	L
D	Panel		L	D	L	D
L	D	L	D	L	D	L
D	L	D	L	D	L	D

Section F

| L |
| D |
| L |
| D |

Section H

| Panel | L |

MAKING THE QUILT TOP

Note: This quilt is built in sections. Once all the individual blocks have been made, three units (top, middle and bottom) will be made, utilizing the individual blocks. Orient all pieced blocks with the longest logs on the left and bottom of the block.

Top Section

1 Gather eleven light and nine dark 8" blocks, four light and four dark 6" blocks, and thirteen light and thirteen dark 4" blocks. Also gather the small 4½" × 8½" panel along with a 16½" × 8½" panel and one of the 20½" × 8½" panels.

2 On a design wall or large flat surface, lay out the blocks for the top section according to the quilt diagram above. Take care to keep the light (L) and dark (D) blocks in an alternating pattern as shown in the diagram.

3 Stitch together the blocks in the top row (Section A) and press the seams toward the dark blocks. Return the row to the design wall.

4 Stitch together the short row of four 8" blocks (Section B) and press the seams toward the dark blocks. Repeat for the two-block-and-panel row (Section C) as well as the other four-block short row (Section D). Press all seams toward the dark blocks.

5 Stitch a four-block row (Section B) to the top of the panel-and-block row (Section C).

6 Add the remaining short four-block row (Section D) to the bottom of that section (Section C) and press all seams down. Return the section to the design wall.

7 Stitch the blocks together in the vertical rows of four 6" blocks (Sections E and F). Stitch both rows and press the seams down. Return the vertical rows to the design wall.

8 Sew the blocks together, row by row, in the 4" block-and-panel section (Section G). Press the seams toward the dark blocks.

9 Join the 4" block rows and press all seams down.

10 Add the 8" light block to the right edge of the 20½" × 8½" panel (Section H) and press the seam toward the panel.

11 Add the panel-block strip (Section H) to the bottom of the 4" block section (Section G) and press the seam down.

12 Stitch a vertical row of 6" blocks (Section E) to the right edge of the 8" block-and-panel section (Section B, C and D). Press the seam toward the larger blocks.

13 Stitch a vertical row of 6" blocks (Section F) to the right edge of the 4" block-and-panel section (Sections G and H) and press the seam toward the larger blocks.

14 Stitch the sections together and press the seam toward the larger blocks.

15 Add the top 8" block row (Section A) and press the seam down. The top section is done!

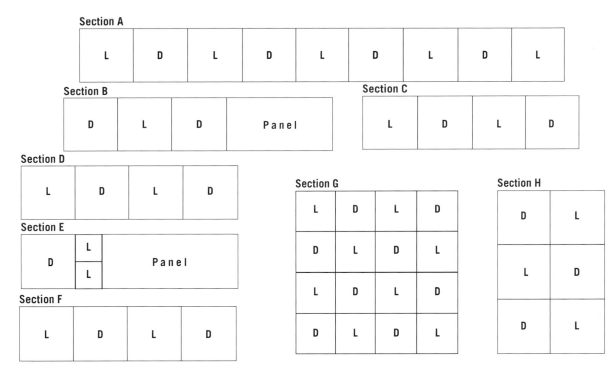

Middle Section

1 Gather the remaining two panels, two light 4" blocks, eight dark and eight light 6" blocks, and fifteen light and sixteen dark 8" blocks. Arrange them on the design wall according to the quilt diagram above.

2 Stitch the blocks together in the alternating 8" block row (Section A). Press the seams toward the dark blocks and return the long row to the design wall.

3 Stitch three 8" blocks together and add the 16½" × 8½" panel to the right edge of that partial row (Section B). Press the seams toward the dark blocks. Stitch the four remaining blocks in that row together (Section C) and join the sections to complete the row. Press the seams toward the dark block.

4 Join the two rows from Steps 2 and 3 (Sections A, B and C) and press the seam down. Return the two-row unit to the design wall.

5 Make two short rows, four blocks each (Sections D and F), of alternating 8" blocks. Press the seams toward the dark blocks and return them to the design wall.

6 Stitch the 4" light blocks together and add them to the right edge of an 8" dark block. Press the seam toward the dark block. Add the final panel to the other 4" block edge and press the seam toward the panel (Section E).

7 Stitch a four-block row (Sections D and F) to the top and bottom of the panel-block row (Section E) and press all seams down. Return the section to the design wall.

8 Create the 6" block checkerboard section by stitching the blocks together (press seams toward the dark blocks) and then joining the four rows (Section G). Press all seams down. Return this unit to the design wall.

9 Stitch the remaining blocks together in the three alternating rows of two 8" blocks each (Section H). Press the seams toward the dark blocks and stitch the three rows together. Press the seams down. Join this to the right edge of the sixteen-block checkerboard of 6" blocks (Section G). Press the seam toward the larger blocks.

10 Add the short three-row unit (Sections D, E and F) with a panel in the middle row to the left side of the sixteen-block checkerboard (Section G and H) and press the seam toward the larger blocks. Stitch the two-row unit from Step 4 (Sections A, B and C) to the top of the section just created. Press the seam down. The middle section is done!

Bottom Section

1 Simply make two alternating rows of the eighteen remaining 8" blocks to complete the bottom section. Press the seams toward the dark blocks.

2 Sew the rows together and press the seam down. Now you're ready to sew all three sections together and press the seams down.

FINISHING THE QUILT

1 Use wool batting for authenticity and warmth in this quilt. The drape and feel of wool is unbeatable in a quilt created to honor the past. The quilted text consists of additional Harriet Tubman quotes—I didn't want her words to be lost, and the texture of wool batting adds emphasis to these words.

Wise Water
72½" × 88½"
Pieced and quilted by the author
Fabrics courtesy of Marcus Fabrics

Wise Water is a modern manipulation of the design and layout of *Wise Words* (page 56). In this adaptation, the places that held panels in *Wise Words* now showcase terrific large-scale prints.

The fluctuating zinger fabrics create the ebb and flow of a calm pool that gives sustenance and provides reflection. I see this quilt as a contemporary expression of the strong foundation women like Harriet Tubman have provided with their wisdom and their words. Powerful words inspire, empower and enlighten us. The clear, strong lines of *Wise Water* reflect that positive path and open the door to further reflection and growth.

FABRIC REQUIREMENTS

Zinger Aqua Tones: ⅛ yd. each of 3 different fabrics

Large-Scale Black with White Print: ⅓ yd.

Large-Scale White with Black Print: ½ yd.

Preprinted Black-and-White with 6" squares: 1¾ yds.

Preprinted Black-and-White with 2¼" Lengthwise Stripes: 4¼ yds.

Black Solid or Tone-on-Tone: ⅛ yd. each of 9 different fabrics

White Solid or Tone-on-Tone: ⅙ yd. each of 6 different fabrics

Binding: ⅞ yd.

Backing: 5¾ yds.

Batting: 80½" × 96½"

CUTTING INSTRUCTIONS

ZINGER AQUA TONES:
Cut 3 strips 1½" (one from each fabric); from these strips:
Cut 6 strips 1½" × 21"

LARGE-SCALE BLACK WITH WHITE PRINT:
Cut 1 strip 8½"; from this strip:
Cut 1 strip 8½" × 20½"
Cut 1 strip 8½" × 16½"

LARGE-SCALE WHITE WITH BLACK PRINT:
Cut 1 strip 8½"; from this strip:
Cut 1 strip 8½" × 20½"
Cut 1 strip 8½" × 16½"
Cut 1 strip 8½" × 4½"

PREPRINTED BLACK-AND-WHITE WITH 6" SQUARES (OR REPLACEMENT FABRIC IF PREPRINTED FABRIC IS NOT AVAILABLE):
Cut 1 strip 24½"; from this strip:
Cut 1 square 24½" × 24½" (4 × 4 checkerboard of preprinted squares, or replace with a 4 × 4 pieced checkerboard if preprinted fabric is not available)
Cut 2 rectangles 24½" × 6½" (4 × 1 row of preprinted squares, or replace with a 4 × 1 pieced row if preprinted fabric is not available)
Fussy-cut 13 dark and 13 light 4½" squares from the center of preprinted squares, or from replacement fabrics if preprinted fabric is not available

CONTINUES ON NEXT PAGE

If Preprinted Fabric Is Not Available

Lightest White: 1½ yds.

Light: 1½ yds.

Medium White: ¾ yd.

Darkest Dark: ½ yd.

Dark: 1½ yds.

Medium Dark: ¾ yd.

Black Solid or Tone-on-Tone: ⅛ yd. each of 9 different fabrics

White Solid or Tone-on-Tone: ⅙ yd. each of 6 different fabrics

PREPRINTED BLACK-AND-WHITE WITH 2¼" LENGTHWISE STRIPES (OR REPLACEMENT FABRIC IF PREPRINTED FABRIC IS NOT AVAILABLE):

Lightest White: Cut into 1½" lengthwise strips; from these strips:

> Cut 11 strips 1½" × 6½"
> Cut 22 strips 1½" × 7½"
> Cut 11 strips 1½" × 8½"

Medium White: Cut into 1½" lengthwise strips; from these strips:

> Cut 3 strips 1½" × 21" from different prints
> Cut 70 strips 1½" × 2½"
> Cut 35 strips 1½" × 3½"

Light (Plus Leftover Lightest Light and Medium Light): Cut into 2" lengthwise strips; from these strips:

> Cut 35 strips 2" × 3½"
> Cut 70 strips 2" × 5"
> Cut 35 strips 2" × 6½"

Darkest Dark: Cut into 1½" lengthwise strips; from these strips:

> Cut 7 strips 1½" × 6½"
> Cut 20 strips 1½" × 7½"
> Cut 13 strips 1½" × 8½"

Medium Dark: Cut into 1½" lengthwise strips; from these strips:

> Cut 3 strips 1½" × 21" from different prints
> Cut 68 strips 1½" × 2½"
> Cut 34 strips 1½" × 3½"

Dark (Plus leftover Darkest Dark and Medium Dark): Cut into 2" lengthwise strips; from these strips:

> Cut 34 strips 2" × 3½"
> Cut 68 strips 2" × 5"
> Cut 34 strips 2" × 6½"

BLACK SOLID OR TONE-ON-TONE:

Cut into 1½" lengthwise strips; from these strips:

> Cut 27 strips 1½" × 6½"
> Cut 48 strips 1½" × 7½"
> Cut 21 strips 1½" × 8½"

WHITE SOLID OR TONE-ON-TONE:

Cut into 1½" lengthwise strips; from these strips:

> Cut 24 strips 1½" × 6½"
> Cut 48 strips 1½" × 7½"
> Cut 12 strips 1½" × 8½"

BINDING

Cut 1 square 29" for 2¼" continuous bias binding

NOTES ON THIS QUILT

Much of the piecing in this project is eliminated by using preprinted squares. This fabulous print has the piecework done for me! The 6" block print is perfect for a 6" block checkerboard with absolutely no piecing.

By cutting apart the preprinted blocks, I used the 4" center section for the 4" blocks. Substituting single blocks with very high contrast updates the design and makes it easy to execute in far less time. The only blocks I pieced are the 8" log cabin blocks.

You might be thinking, "But what a waste of fabric!" Not so. Save those strips of black and white and piece them into a fantastic checkerboard for another project! They will make a stunning border with half the work. *That* is clever piecing!

Another time-saver is using a fabric that has varied prints in lengthwise stripes. Because the fabric designer used a variety of scales, the fabric selection and careful shopping are done for us. The strips will be cut apart lengthwise to yield a wonderful array of prints. This type of piecing is not cheating—it is streamlining and working smarter! Just add a few zinger fabrics for contrast, emphasis and punch, and voilà! You've created a stunning quilt with a simplified design.

Preprinted Squares

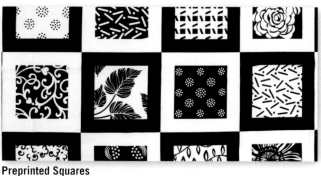

Fabrics with Varied Prints in Lengthwise Strips

Zinger Fabrics

CONSTRUCTING THE 8½" LIGHT BLOCKS

Note: Throughout this pattern the blocks will be referred to by their cut size, not by their finished size:

1 Layer a 1½" × 21" medium light strip, right sides together, with a 1½" × 21" aqua strip and stitch together.

2 Piece each remaining medium light strip to a different aqua strip.

3 Press the seam allowances toward the medium light strips.

4 Cut the strip sets into thirty-five segments 1½" wide.

5 Move the segments to the left of the sewing machine, along with the 2½" strips of the matching medium light fabric.

6 Add a 1½" × 2½" medium light strip and stitch. Always put on the bottom the piece that has already been sewn and layer the new strip on top. Also make sure the strip that was just added is fed through the machine first. This guarantees the logs will go around the center the same way every time. Repeat for all thirty-five light blocks.

7 Press the seams out toward the medium light strip.

8 Using a different medium light fabric, add a 2½" medium light log to each block, followed by a 3½" medium light log of the same fabric. Press the seams out.

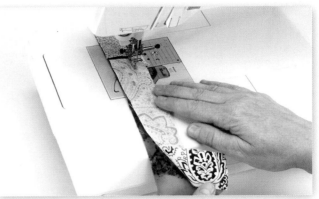

CONSTRUCTING THE 8½" LIGHT BLOCKS **Step 1**

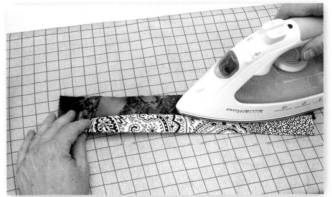

CONSTRUCTING THE 8½" LIGHT BLOCKS **Step 3**

CONSTRUCTING THE 8½" LIGHT BLOCKS **Step 4**

CONSTRUCTING THE 8½" LIGHT BLOCKS **Step 5**

CONSTRUCTING THE 8½" LIGHT BLOCKS **Step 8**

9 Next, add a 2" × 3½" light log, remembering to put the previously sewn log into the machine first with the new log on top. Add a 2" × 5" light log of the same fabric and press the seams out.

10 Choose 5" and 6½" logs of another light fabric and add them to finish the ring. Press the seams out.

11 Complete the block by adding the final lightest light ring of logs, making sure the 6½" and 7½" logs are the same fabric. Choose a different fabric for the 7½" and 8½" logs, add to the block and press the seams out.

12 Repeat this process for all thirty-five light 8½" blocks.

CONSTRUCTING THE 8½" LIGHT BLOCKS **Step 9**

CONSTRUCTING THE 8½" DARK BLOCKS

1 Layer a 1½" × 21" medium dark strip, right sides together, with an aqua 1½" × 21" strip and stitch together.

2 Piece the remaining medium dark strips with aqua strips.

3 Press the seam allowances toward the medium dark strips.

4 Cut the strip sets into thirty-four segments 1½" wide.

CONSTRUCTING THE 8½" LIGHT BLOCKS **Step 10**

5 Move the segments to the left of the sewing machine, along with the 2½" strips of matching medium dark.

6 Add a 1½" × 2½" medium dark strip and stitch. Always put on the bottom the piece that has already been sewn and layer the new strip on top. Also make sure the strip that was just added is fed through the machine first. This guarantees the logs will go around the center the same way every time. Repeat for all thirty-four dark blocks and press the seams out toward the medium dark strip.

CONSTRUCTING THE 8½" LIGHT BLOCKS **Step 11**

CONSTRUCTING THE 8½" DARK BLOCKS **Step 7**

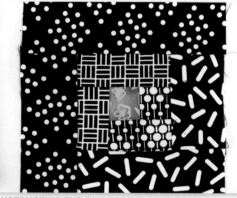

CONSTRUCTING THE 8½" DARK BLOCKS **Step 9**

7 Using a different medium dark fabric, add a 2½" medium dark log to each block, followed by a 3½" medium dark log of the same fabric. Repeat for all blocks and press the seams out.

8 Next, add a 2" × 3½" dark log, remembering to put the previously sewn log into the machine first with the new log on top. Add a 2" × 5" dark log of the same fabric and press the seams out.

9 Choose 5" and 6½" logs of another dark fabric and add them to finish the ring. Press the seams out.

10 Complete the block by adding the final ring of darkest dark logs, making sure the 6½" and 7½" logs are the same fabric. Choose a different fabric for the 7½" and 8½" logs and add to the block.

11 Repeat this process for all thirty-four dark 8½" blocks.

CONSTRUCTING THE 8½" DARK BLOCKS Step10

Section A

D	L	D	L	D	L	D	L	D

Section B

L	D	L	D

Section C

D	L	8½" × 16½" Large-Scale Black with White Print

Section D

L	D	L	D

Section E

preprinted square
preprinted square
preprinted square
preprinted square

Section F

D	L	D	L	D	L	D
L	8½" × 4½" White with Black Print	D	L	D	L	
D	L	D	L	D	L	D
L	D	L	D	L	D	L

Section H

8½" × 20½" Large-Scale White with Black Print	D

Section G

preprinted square
preprinted square
preprinted square
preprinted square

MAKING THE QUILT TOP

Note: This quilt is built in sections. Once all the individual 8½" blocks have been made, three units (top, middle, and bottom) will be put together, utilizing the pieced blocks, the very large print panel blocks, the checkerboard preprinted section and the 4½" fussy-cut blocks. Orient all pieced blocks with the 7½" and 8½" logs on the left and bottom of the block.

Top Section

1 Gather eleven dark 8½" blocks, nine light 8½" blocks, two preprinted rows of four 6½" blocks and thirteen each of light and dark 4½" squares. Also gather the 4½" × 8½" large-scale white with black print, the 8½" × 16½" large-scale black with white print and the 8½" × 20½" large-scale white with black print.

2 On a design wall or large flat surface, lay out the blocks for the top section according to the quilt diagram above. Take care to arrange the light and dark blocks in an alternating pattern, as seen in the diagram above.

3 Stitch together the five dark, alternating with four light, 8½" pieced blocks in the top row (Section A on page 71) and press the seams toward the dark blocks. Return the row to the very top of the design wall.

4 Stitch together a short row of two dark, alternating with two light, 8½" pieced blocks (Section B on page 71) and press the seams toward the dark blocks. Repeat to make a total of two rows of four blocks (Sections B and D on page 71).

5 Create the next row by adding a light 8½" block to the right edge of a dark 8½" block. Press the seams toward the dark block and add the dark 8½"x 16½" large-scale black with white print to the right edge of the light block (Section C on page 71). Press the seam toward the panel.

6 Join the rows formed in Steps 4–5 together, sandwiching the row from Step 5 (Section C) between 2 four-block rows (Sections B and D). Press the seams down and return the section to the design wall.

7 Sew the 4½" fussy-cut alternating blocks and the 4½" × 8½" large-scale white with black print together, row by row, in the 4½" block section (Section F on page 71). Press the seams toward the dark blocks.

8 Join the 4½" block rows to make a checkerboard section of 4 rows by 7 blocks and press all seams down.

9 Sew an 8½" pieced dark block to the right edge of the 8½" × 20½" large-scale white with black print (Section H on page 71) and press the seam toward the panel.

10 Add the strip from Step 9 to the bottom of the 4½" checkerboard section and press the seam down.

11 Stitch a vertical row of preprinted 6½" blocks (Sections E and G on page 71) to each side of the unit made in Step 10 (Sections F and H). Press the seams out toward the preprinted blocks.

12 Join the section just made (Sections E, F and H) to the right edge of the 8½" pieced blocks-and-panel unit (Sections B, C and D). Press the seam toward the vertical row of preprinted 6½" blocks.

13 Add the top 8½" pieced block row (Section A) and press the seam down. The top section is complete and can be returned to the design wall.

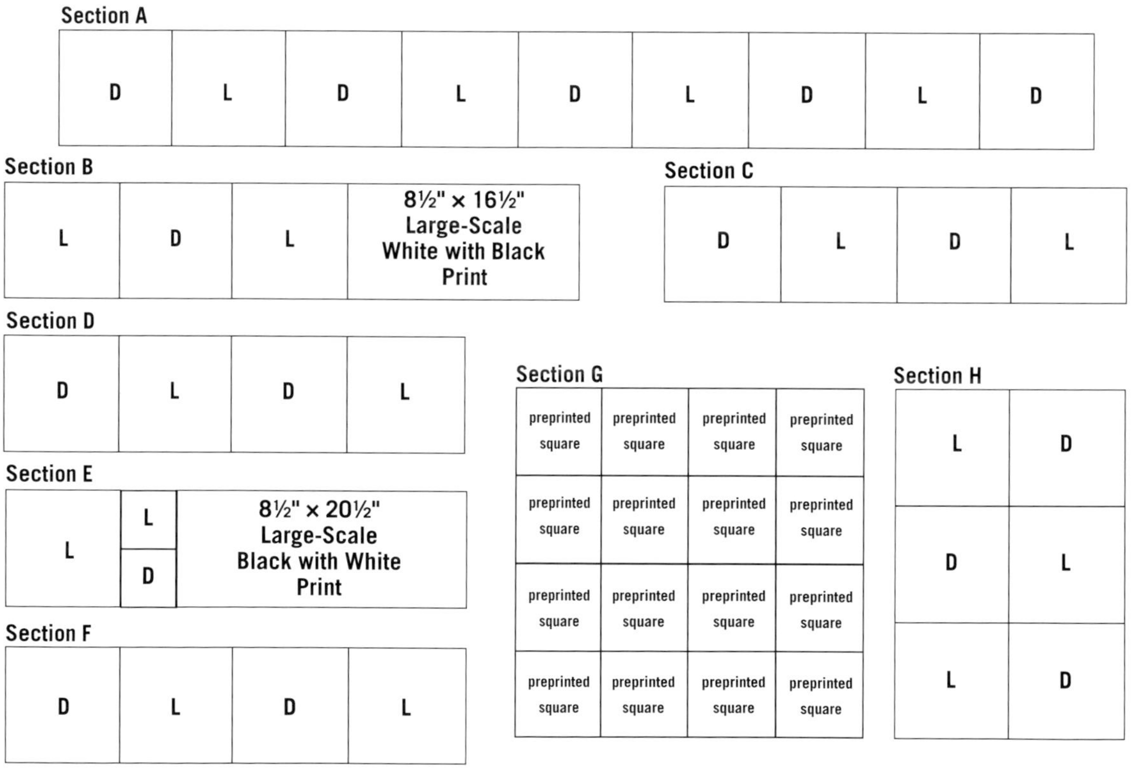

Section A

D	L	D	L	D	L	D	L	D

Section B

L	D	L	8½" × 16½" Large-Scale White with Black Print

Section C

D	L	D	L

Section D

D	L	D	L

Section E

L	L / D	8½" × 20½" Large-Scale Black with White Print

Section F

D	L	D	L

Section G

preprinted square	preprinted square	preprinted square	preprinted square
preprinted square	preprinted square	preprinted square	preprinted square
preprinted square	preprinted square	preprinted square	preprinted square
preprinted square	preprinted square	preprinted square	preprinted square

Section H

L	D
D	L
L	D

Middle Section

1 Gather the remaining two panels, one dark and one light, two 4½" blocks, the preprinted 4 × 4 checkerboard of 6½" blocks and sixteen light and fifteen dark 8½" blocks. Arrange them on the design wall according to the quilt diagram above.

2 Stitch nine blocks together in the alternating 8½" block row, starting with a dark block (Section A above). Press the seams toward the dark blocks and return the long row to the design wall.

3 Sandwich a dark 8½" block between two light 8½" blocks and stitch to make a short alternating row. Add the 8½" × 16½" large-scale white with black print to the right edge of that short row and press the seams toward the dark blocks (Section B on page 72).

4 Stating with a dark block, stitch an alternating row of two dark and two light 8½" blocks (Section C on page 72). Stitch that row to the right edge of the 8½" × 16½" large-scale white with black print. Press the seams toward the dark blocks.

5 Join the two rows from Steps 2–4 (Sections A, B and C) and press the seam down. Return the two-row unit to the design wall.

6 Make two short vertical rows, four blocks each, alternating light and dark 8½" blocks (Sections D and F on page 72). Start with a dark block on both rows. Press the seams toward the dark blocks and return them to the design wall.

7 Stitch the 4½" light and dark blocks together and add them to the right edge of an 8½" light block. The light 4½" block should be on top of the dark block. Press the seam toward the 4½" block. Add the final 8½" × 20½" large-scale black with white print to the 4½" block edge and press the seam toward the large block (Section E on page 72).

8 Stitch a four-block row (Sections D and F) to the top and bottom of the row from Step 7 (Section E) and press all seams down. Return the section to the design wall.

9 Sew a dark 8½" block to the right edge of a light 8½" block. Repeat to make a total of two sets. Press seams to the dark blocks.

10 Sew a light 8½" block to the right edge of a dark 8½" block. Press the seam towards the dark block and join the three rows together by sandwiching the dark-light set between the two light-dark sets (Section H on page 72). Press the seams down.

11 Join this three-row unit (Section H) to the right edge of the preprinted checkerboard of 6½" blocks (Section G). Press the seam toward the preprinted panel.

12 Add the three-row unit from Step 8 (Sections D, E and F) to the left side of the preprinted checkerboard and press the seam toward the checkerboard.

13 Stitch the two-row unit from Step 5 (Sections A, B and C) to the top of the section just created. Press the seam down. The middle is done!

L	D	L	D	L	D	L	D	L
D	L	D	L	D	L	D	L	D

Bottom Section

1 Simply make two alternating rows of the eighteen remaining 8½" blocks to complete the bottom section. One row will begin with a light block, and the bottom row will begin with a dark block. Press seams toward the dark blocks.

2 Sew the rows together and press the seam down. Could that have been any easier?

PUTTING THE QUILT TOP TOGETHER

1 Sew all three sections together and press the seams down.

FINISHING THE QUILT

1 When quilting a piece with this much block and print activity, the quilting would have to be very strong and in a vastly contrasting color to take center stage. Instead of trying to compete with the design and fabrics, the quilting can add texture and definition to sections of the quilt. Separate the quilt top into areas of texture instead of thinking in terms of an entire quilting design for the top as a whole. Most importantly, play with texture to enhance and highlight the wonderful fabrics you've chosen for your quilt!

Fractured Flowers
36½" × 36½"
Pieced and quilted by the author

Every so often I come across a piece of fabric so unlike what I normally select that I just can't put it down! The spaced floral used for this quilt was definitely one of those fabrics. It has more than one color, which can scare me, and has very little black. The vivid contrast I crave is present, but the value change is one big leap! There is no print to work with, just very large blossoms.

The vivid colors drew me in and challenged me to find a way to incorporate these highly individual blossoms into a simple, yet very structured wall hanging. Oh, and there is pink involved as well! A very dear friend of mine is enamored with pinks. Amaranth, cerise, magenta, carnation, cherry blossom, classic rose, mauve, mulberry, coral, tea rose, pastel, hot pink—you name it—she has it in her fabric collection. Spurred on by her love of the color, I rose to the challenge not only to use the pink flowers, but to add a soft, metallic pink dot to the mix as well. *Fractured Flowers* is the simple, yet beautiful outcome of my experimentation.

FABRIC REQUIREMENTS

Large Flower Print: 3 repeats of the flower motif

White with Pink Metallic Dots: ⅓ yd.

Small-Scale Black with White Leaves: ⅓ yd.

Medium-Scale Black with White Print: ¼ yd.

Small-Scale Black-and-White Tile: ¼ yd.

Intense Pink Zinger: ¼ yd.

Large-Scale Black Anemone: ¾ yd.

Black with White Dot-Stripe: ⅝ yd.

Backing: 1¼ yds.

Batting: 44½" × 44½"

CUTTING INSTRUCTIONS

LARGE FLOWER PRINT:
Cut 1 square 11" with flower centered
Cut 2 squares 8½" with flower centered

WHITE WITH PINK METALLIC DOTS:
Cut 1 square 11"

SMALL-SCALE BLACK WITH WHITE LEAVES:
Cut 3 strips 2"
Cut 3 strips 1½"

MEDIUM-SCALE BLACK WITH WHITE PRINT:
Cut 3 strips 2"

SMALL-SCALE BLACK-AND-WHITE TILE:
Cut 3 strips 1½"

INTENSE PINK ZINGER:
Cut 3 strips 1½"

LARGE-SCALE BLACK ANEMONE:
Cut 4 strips 5½"; from these strips:
    Cut 2 strips 5½" × 26½"
    Cut 2 strips 5½" × 36½"

BLACK WITH WHITE DOT-STRIPE:
Cut 1 square 20" for 2¼" continuous-bias binding

Balancing the Florals with Black-and-White Prints

Measuring the Blossoms

Cutting the Fabric

NOTES ON THIS QUILT

Even though I welcomed the challenge of working with fabrics and colors that aren't my typical choice, for my sanity I had to toss in some very bold black-and-white prints to balance the flower and intense zinger. The wide-scale variety in the prints will add movement, interest and the needed variations in value.

The first step is always to measure the panel or motif you are working with. The blossoms measure 7" across, so the goal is to end up with a finished block of 8". That will allow for a little white space around the blossom, but won't blind us with shocking white.

Because the flowers are circular, divided segments will create pinwheels. The rounded edges will maintain a circular feel, while separating the sections will add more negative space and create two blocks from one motif. What a way to be thrifty!

The very light background is perfect to feature the flowers and balance a dark, active border. Adding only single-fabric borders to this motif would not utilize its potential. By piecing more intricate layers around the motifs, they can sparkle and completely pop without overwhelming a simplistic and too-basic and frame.

PREPARING THE FLOWER

1 Layer the 11" flower square, right sides together, on the 11" white with pink dot square. Cut the layered blocks in half diagonally, from point to point. Repeat by cutting diagonally in line with the opposite points. Do not move the layers.

2 Cut again down the vertical center of the block. Each half will measure 5½". Rotate the mat 90° and cut the block perpendicularly to the vertical center cut. Once again the halves will measure 5½".

3 Carefully move the layered segments to the left of the sewing machine. Stitch each segment together on the diagonal edge. Keep the flower print on top and feed the flower point through the machine first on all segments. Repeat for all eight segments.

4 Press the seams toward the flower section. This may seem odd, but pressing the seam allowances this way will put the extra layers under the floral pinwheel when the piece is quilted. The added thickness will help lift the pinwheel off the front of the quilt, and the lack of extra layers will allow the background to recede.

5 Half the quarter blocks will have the flower section on the left, and the other half will be on the right. Separate the like quarter blocks and use one set for each pinwheel block. Lay out the quarter blocks as they will appear in the quilt.

6 Layer the top two quarter blocks right sides together and nestle the diagonal seams. Stitch together. Repeat by chain piecing the three remaining sets.

7 Press the half blocks open with the seam allowances toward the flower sections.

8 Layer the like half blocks, right sides together, and nestle the seams carefully in the center. Stitch together to create a block.

9 Repeat for the other pinwheel block and press the blocks open. At first glance, the pinwheel blocks will appear to be the same but they are mirror images.

10 Square the pinwheel blocks to 8½".

PREPARING THE FLOWER **Step 1**

PREPARING THE FLOWER **Step 2**

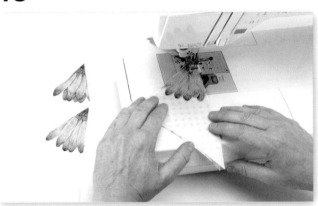

PREPARING THE FLOWER **Step 3**

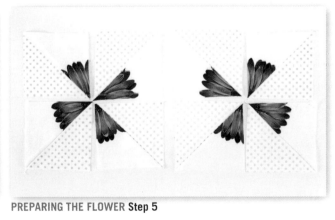

PREPARING THE FLOWER **Step 5**

PREPARING THE FLOWER **Step 8**

PREPARING THE FLOWER **Step 10**

CREATING THE QUILT CENTER **Step 1**

CREATING THE QUILT CENTER

1 Pair up a pinwheel block with an 8½" single-floral block. Layer the blocks right sides together and stitch. Repeat for the remaining pair of blocks. Press the seams toward the single-floral blocks.

2 Layer the rows, right sides together, with the pinwheel blocks facing single-floral blocks. Nestle the seams together.

3 Hold the nestled seams firmly as you sew the two rows together. Stitch and press the rows open. The center of the quilt can be set aside for now.

MAKING THE INNER BORDER

1 Line up stacks of the black-and-white print strips in piecing order.

2 Layer a 2" leaf print strip on top of a 2" black medium print strip, right sides together; stitch the strips together.

3 Layer the 1½" black-and-white tile print strip on top of the other side of the 2" leaf print strip and stitch.

4 Press all seams toward the darker end of the strip set.

5 Repeat Steps 1–4 for all three strip sets.

6 Cut a total of twenty segments 4½" wide.

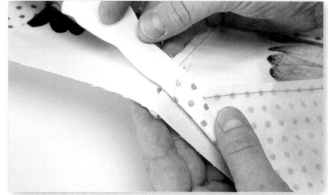
CREATING THE QUILT CENTER **Step 2**

CREATING THE QUILT CENTER **Step 3**

MAKING THE INNER BORDER **Step 1**

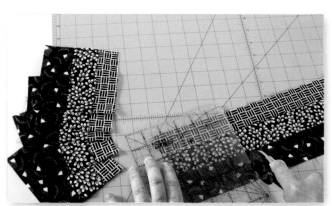
MAKING THE INNER BORDER **Step 6**

7 With twelve of the segments, create two rows of six segments each. Both rows will have the strips vertical and the darkest strip on the left side. Layer two segments, keeping the strips vertical and the darkest strip on the left on the bottom segment. Stitch together. Repeat for a total of six pairs. Press the seams toward the darkest strip.

8 Layer two of the two-block units, right sides together, and stitch. Repeat to create a second unit of four blocks.

9 Add a two-block unit to the end of each four-block unit and press the seams toward the darkest strip. These two rows are the top and bottom inner borders.

10 The remaining eight blocks will be used to make the alternating side borders. Lay two strip blocks together, end to end, with the darkest strips on opposite sides.

11 Layer the two blocks, right sides together, and stitch. Remember that the seams will not match up because the strips are different widths. How is that for making your life easy? Repeat for four sets of two blocks each.

12 Combine two sets, end to end, to make a complete side border. Layer the two-block units, right sides together, and sew. Repeat for the remaining two sets. Press the seams all one way.

13 Stitch the side inner borders to each side of the quilt center and press the seams out. Add the top and bottom inner borders to the quilt center and press the seams out. Set the quilt center aside for now.

MAKING THE INNER BORDER Step 7

MAKING THE INNER BORDER Step 10

MAKING THE INNER BORDER Step 13

PIECING THE MIDDLE BORDER Step 1

PIECING THE MIDDLE BORDER Step 2

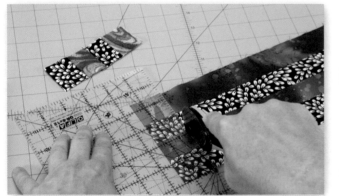

PIECING THE MIDDLE BORDER Step 4

PIECING THE MIDDLE BORDER

1 Layer a 1½" zinger strip on top of a 1½" black-and-white with leaf print strip, right sides together. Stitch the strips together. Press the seam allowance toward the black print strip. Repeat for a total of three strip sets.

2 From one strip set, cut two segments 1½" wide. Set these aside for the top and bottom middle borders. Cut the remainder of that strip set in half to yield two 20" strips.

3 Join the two full-length strip sets to create a four-strip set. Layer the sets right sides together and join the black leaf print strip to the edge of the zinger in the other strip set. Press the seams toward the black print strip. Join the two half-strip sets in the same manner.

4 Cut a total of twenty-four segments 1½" wide.

5 Stitch the checkerboard units together, alternating end to end, to make four strips of six units each. Press the seams toward the dark squares.

6 Add a two-patch unit from Step 2 to the end of one strip. Add the remaining two-patch unit to the end of another strip. Press the seams toward the dark squares. These are the top and bottom middle borders.

7 Line up a checkerboard strip, without the added two-patch unit, to the right edge of the quilt. Put a zinger square at the top right corner. Nestle the seams every 4" at the corners of the strip blocks and sew the right-side middle border to the quilt.

8 Line up the remaining checkerboard block, without the added two-patch unit, with the left side of the quilt. Put a black print square in the upper left corner. Nestle the seams every 4" at the corners of the strip blocks and sew the left-side middle border to the quilt. Press both seams toward the inner border.

9 Stitch the upper middle border to the top of the quilt, with a zinger square in the upper left corner.

10 Stitch the bottom middle border to the bottom of the quilt, with a black print square in the bottom left position to maintain the alternating checkerboard. Press both seams toward the inner border.

PIECING THE MIDDLE BORDER Step 5

MAKING THE OUTER BORDER

1 Stitch the 5½" × 26½" black anemone print strips to the sides of the quilt and press the seams out.

2 Stitch the 5½" × 36½" black anemone print strips to the top and bottom of the quilt and press the seams out.

FINISHING THE QUILT

1 It is time to layer, quilt and bind our work. For this piece, I maximized the floral motif by quilting leaves around the single flowers. This dense quilting gives wonderful texture and light variations to the white background.

2 To contrast the floral blocks, I quilted straight lines, emphasizing the pinwheel effect, yet giving a hint of the flower by completing a few petals and creating the centers on the pinwheel flowers.

3 The quilting on the multiple borders purposely does not compete with the quilt center. The frame is there to support the middle but not detract from it.

4 The zippy dot-stripe binding on the bias gives the suggestion that this floral tile could go on and on and on. Just whose garden is it?

MAKING THE OUTER BORDER Step 2

FINISHING THE QUILT Step 1

FINISHING THE QUILT Step 2

inchworm

Inchworm
48½" × 72½"
Pieced and quilted by the author
Fabrics courtesy of Island Batiks, Inc.

I hear a lot about quilt guilds and groups doing "Challenge Quilts." I absolutely love that idea and wanted to do one myself. What rule did I want to break? What hurdle did I want to tackle? I decided to defy one of my self-imposed quilting rules. Normally, I don't use the positive and negative of the same print in one quilt, but I wanted to see if I could create a quilt in which the two prints would accentuate one another without screaming, "We are the same print!" *Inchworm* is the result of that test. I pushed myself to use not only a large black medium value floral print in the piecing and the border—another challenge for me—but also to use the reverse print, a very light white/gray version in the piecing as well.

As is often the case, it took several tries to strike the right balance for the overall design of *Inchworm*. In this sense, quilting is like playing with building blocks: Some creations stand tall the first time, and some take repeated effort to achieve the right combination of units. As such, don't fret if things don't fall into place right away. Keep playing until your internal monitor signals you to stop. Your gut is always your most valuable design tool.

FABRIC REQUIREMENTS

White Large Floral Batik: 2¼ yds.

Black-and-White Large Floral Batik: 2⅝ yds.

Black-and-White Medium Floral Batik: ¾ yd.

Black-and-White Small Leaves Batik: ⅓ yd.

Black-and-White Large Leaves Batik: ⅙ yd.

Black-and-White Branches Batik: ⅛ yd.

Black with White Knobby Stripe Batik: 1 yd.

Solid Black Batik: ⅛ yd.

Zinger Green Batik: ½ yd.

Backing: 4 yds.

Batting: 56½" × 80½"

CUTTING INSTRUCTIONS

WHITE LARGE FLORAL BATIK:
Cut 6 strips 3½"
Cut 1 strip 1½"
Cut 1 strip 1¼"

BLACK-AND-WHITE LARGE FLORAL BATIK:
Cut 2 lengthwise strips 6½" × 18½"
Cut 2 lengthwise strips 6½" × 30½"
Cut 1 lengthwise strip 6½" × 36½"

BLACK-AND-WHITE MEDIUM FLORAL BATIK:
Cut 6 strips 3½"

BLACK-AND-WHITE SMALL LEAVES BATIK:
Cut 3 strips 2½"

BLACK-AND-WHITE LARGE LEAVES BATIK:
Cut 2 strips 2"

BLACK-AND-WHITE BRANCHES BATIK:
Cut 1 strip 1"

BLACK WITH WHITE KNOBBY STRIPE BATIK:
Cut 2 strips 1½"
Cut 1 square 26" for 2¼" continuous bias binding

SOLID BLACK BATIK:
Cut 3 strips 1"

ZINGER GREEN BATIK:
Cut 1 strip 1"
Cut 5 strips 1¼"
Cut 2 strips 1½"

Determining the Block Size

Selecting Additional Fabrics

Piecing with a Green Strip

NOTES ON THIS QUILT

For this quilt, I wanted the large print as a focal point for sizable blocks mixed with smaller design elements. To determine the block size, I measured the largest blossom and evaluated what would make the most interesting block. I ended up with a 6½" square, with the largest flower a bit off-center. These blocks will be fussy-cut. Because the large floral design runs lengthwise on the fabric, the print will look best with lengthwise border strips. Thankfully, batik fabrics rip beautifully, so I can rip the lengthwise border strips. That will make up for the tedious fussy-cutting!

With the 6½" block as my common denominator, my experiment turns to breaking up the 6½" block into design units to mix and match and rearrange until the quilt takes shape. Additional fabrics also factor into this equation. With two strong prints as the base, I needed additional prints that were varied in scale, value and style. Different sizes of leaves, bare branches, dotty lines, another floral and solid black add richness and variety to this controlled experiment.

Always a favorite of mine, the four-patch became the first element. As I was cutting the segments for the four-patches, the long shape of the light and dark fabric pieced together intrigued me. What if I used the fabrics for the four-patch but kept them as rectangles? The second element became a block of two 3½" × 6½" strips, one light and one dark.

Because I like uneven patterns, the elements, four-patches, rectangles and 6½" blocks were enough building blocks to play with. I did, however, need to introduce the zinger into the center of the quilt, so I started piecing various strips together with a green strip thrown in. I loved that strippy look so much I pieced segments for the border as well.

MAKING THE UNIT BLOCKS

1 Layer a 3½" white strip right sides together with a 3½" black-and-white medium floral strip and stitch together lengthwise. Repeat to create six strip sets.

2 Set the seams and press toward the black floral.

3 Move the strips to the cutting table and cut eighteen segments 6½" wide. Also cut thirty-two segments 3½" wide.

4 To make the four-patch blocks, nestle two 3½" segments, right sides together, and stitch to make a four-patch. Continue chain piecing for a total of sixteen four-patch blocks; then snip the threads and press the blocks open.

5 Fussy-cut thirteen squares 6½" × 6½" from the white floral, and eight squares 6½" × 6½" from the large black floral.

MAKING THE STRIPPY BLOCKS

Note: There are two different strippy blocks to construct. The 6½" block has five strips, and the 12½" block has eleven strips.

6½" Block

1 Layer a white 1½" strip right sides together with a 2½" black-and-white small leaf strip and stitch them together lengthwise.

2 Add a 2" black large leaf strip to the right edge of the white strip.

3 Add a green 1½" strip to the black large leaf side, followed by a solid black 1" strip. Press the seams one way.

4 Straighten one edge of the strip set and cut six segments 6½" wide. Square the segment to 6½" if necessary.

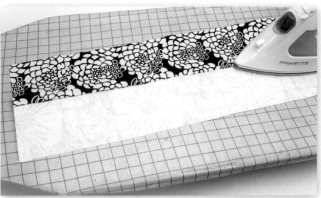

MAKING THE UNIT BLOCKS **Step 2**

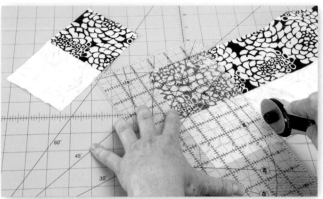

MAKING THE UNIT BLOCKS **Step 3**

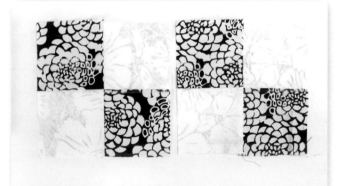

MAKING THE UNIT BLOCKS **Step 4**

MAKING THE STRIPPY BLOCKS **Step 2**

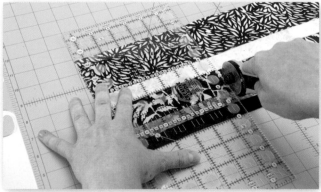

MAKING THE STRIPPY BLOCKS **Step 4**

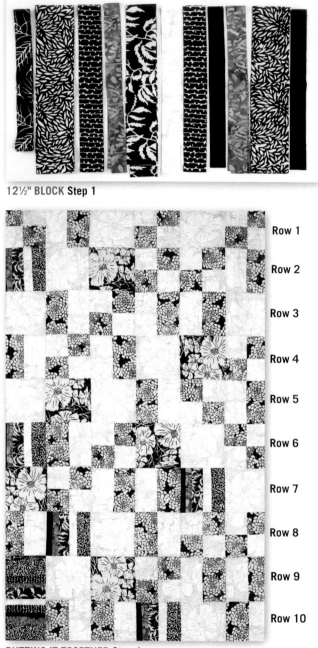

12½" BLOCK Step 1

PUTTING IT TOGETHER Step 1

Row 1
Row 2
Row 3
Row 4
Row 5
Row 6
Row 7
Row 8
Row 9
Row 10

12½" Block

1 Lay out the strips needed for the 12½" block in the order shown at left. Stitch the strips together in that order to make one complete strip set. Press the seams all one way.

2 Straighten one edge of the strip set and cut six segments 6½" wide. Trim the segments to 6½" × 12½" if necessary.

PUTTING IT TOGETHER

1 Following the quilt diagram at left, lay out each of the rows on a design wall. Stitch the blocks together, row by row, until Row 9.

2 Press the seams in alternating directions by row. Rows 1, 3, 5 and 7 press to the right; press Rows 2, 4, 6 and 8 to the left. This will allow the seams to nestle together and make crisp corners.

3 Join the five 6½" blocks in Row 9 and press the seams to the right. Repeat for Row 10 and press the seams to the left.

4 Stitch together Rows 9 and 10 and press the seam down. Add a 12½" vertical block to the left end of the double row and press all seams.

5 Join Rows 1 and 2. Continue by joining Rows 3 and 4, 5 and 6, and 7 and 8.

6 Press all seams down.

7 Stitch the top two double rows together by joining Rows 2 and 3. Repeat by joining Rows 6 and 7.

8 Add the bottom double row to the edge of Row 8, then join the two halves at Rows 4 and 5. Press all seams down.

ADDING THE ZINGER BORDER

1 Cut the ends of all five 1¼" zinger strips at a 45° angle.

2 Layer two ends, right sides together, and sew a ¼" seam. Repeat to make one long strip of zinger.

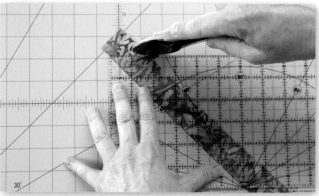

ADDING THE ZINGER BORDER Step 1

3 Press the seams open and then press the entire strip in half, wrong sides together.

4 Cut two strips 36½" and two strips 60½". Stitch the 36½" strips to the bottom and top of the quilt with an ⅛" seam allowance, lining up the cut edges.

5 Layer a 60½" zinger strip on one side of the quilt, on top of the ends of the zinger strips already there. Stitch with an ⅛" seam allowance. Repeat for the other side of the quilt. Do not press the zinger out.

ADDING THE OUTER BORDER

1 Create the bottom border by sandwiching a 12½" strippy block with a 6½" × 18½" black-and-white large floral batik border strip on the left and a 6½" fussy-cut black block on the right. Sew and press the seams away from the strippy block.

2 Stitch this border to the bottom of the quilt, sandwiching the zinger border. Press the border out, being careful to keep the zinger flat against the quilt center.

3 Sew the 36½" × 6½" black-and-white large floral batik border strip to the top of the quilt and carefully press the border out.

4 Sew together the left-side border units consisting of a 6½" × 18½" border strip, a 12½" strippy block, a 6½" × 30½" black-and-white large floral batik border strip and end with a 12½" strippy block (see the photo on page 82 for layout guidance). Press the seams toward the border strips. Add the left-side border to the quilt and carefully press the border out.

5 The right-side border starts with a four-patch block on the end of a 12½" strippy block with a black 6½" block on the other side of the strippy block.
Add a 6½" strippy block to the other side of the dark 6½" block, followed by a 6½" × 30½" border strip. The last piece is a 12½" strippy block on the other end of the border strip (see the photo on page 82 for layout guidance). Sew all together and press the seams away from the strippy blocks.

6 Add the final border and carefully press the seam out.

FINISHING THE QUILT

1 To finish, layer, quilt and bind *Inchworm*.

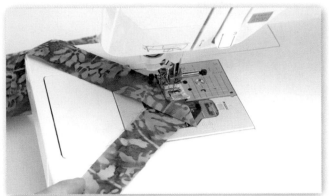
ADDING THE ZINGER BORDER **Step 2**

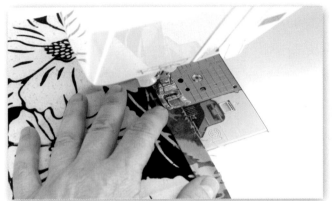
ADDING THE ZINGER BORDER **Step 4**

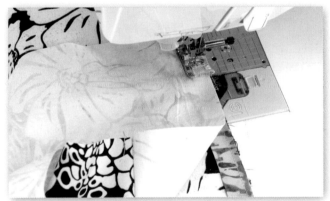
ADDING THE OUTER BORDER **Step 2**

ADDING THE OUTER BORDER **Step 6**

Stripe It Stunning
90⅛" × 104⅝"
Pieced and quilted by the author
Fabrics courtesy of Marcus Fabrics

Once in a while, a fabric company comes up with a great new idea: This quilt uses one of those great ideas, making it simple, fast and so much fun.

The main fabric is printed in lengthwise stripes, which are a fabulous springboard to a host of projects. Having the shopping work done for me really allowed me to be creative with a traditional idea.

I don't usually choose just one line of fabric with one manufacturer, so I found this adventure with a line of fabric surprisingly fun because of the fabric "pencils" it contains. Not only is there a wide variety of value, high contrast and scale changes, but the designs are a collection of contemporary and old-fashioned prints that work beautifully together. If I can't "draw" a quilt with these building blocks, I'm in trouble!

FABRIC REQUIREMENTS

Preprinted Black-and-White Stripe: 5¾ yds.

Purple Zinger: ⅓ yd.

White with Black Leaves: 1¾ yds.

White with Black Paisley: 1½ yds.

Black with Large White Anemone: 1½ yds.

Black with Large White Dot: 1⅛ yds.

Binding: 1 yd.

Backing: 8¼ yds.

Batting: 98" × 113"

CUTTING INSTRUCTIONS

PREPRINTED BLACK-AND-WHITE STRIPE:

Cut 69 strips 2⅞"

PURPLE ZINGER:

Cut 6 strips 1½"; from these strips:
- Cut 70 strips 1½" × 2⅞"

WHITE WITH BLACK LEAVES:

Cut 21 strips 2⅞"; from these strips:
- Cut 2 strips 2⅞" × 3"
- Cut 4 strips 2⅞" × 5⅜"
- Cut 4 strips 2⅞" × 7¾"
- Cut 4 strips 2⅞" × 10⅛"
- Cut 4 strips 2⅞" × 12½"
- Cut 4 strips 2⅞" × 14⅞"
- Cut 4 strips 2⅞" × 17¼"
- Cut 4 strips 2⅞" × 19⅝"
- Cut 4 strips 2⅞" × 22"
- Cut 4 strips 2⅞" × 24⅜"
- Cut 4 strips 2⅞" × 18¾"
- Cut 4 strips 2⅞" × 17⅛"
- Cut 4 strips 2⅞" × 14½"

WHITE WITH BLACK PAISLEY:

Cut 17 strips 2⅞"; from these strips:
- Cut 4 strips 2⅞" × 8½"
- Cut 4 strips 2⅞" × 12½"
- Cut 4 strips 2⅞" × 17½"
- Cut 4 strips 2⅞" × 33⅞"
- Cut 4 strips 2⅞" × 36¼"
- Cut 4 strips 2⅞" × 38⅝"

BLACK WITH LARGE WHITE ANEMONE:

Cut 1 strip 3¾"; from this strip:
- Cut 1 strip 3¾" × 4⅞"
- Cut 2 strips 2⅞" × 6⅛"

Cut 5 strips 8½"; from these strips:
- Cut 3 strips 8½" × 41"

BLACK WITH LARGE WHITE DOT:

Cut 1 strip 3¾"; from this strip:
- Cut 1 strip 3¾" × 4⅞"
- Cut 2 strips 2⅞" × 6⅛"

Cut 3 strips 8½"; from these strips:
- Cut 1 strip 8½" × 41"

BINDING:

Cut 1 square 32" for 2¼" continuous bias binding

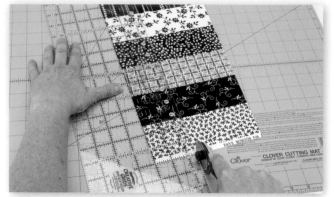

Cutting Cross-Grained Strips

NOTES ON THIS QUILT

I chose a fabric with various prints in lengthwise stripes for the main fabric of this quilt. There are eighteen strips of sixteen different fabrics. With only two repeats and a wide variety of scales and values, this is the beginning of a black-and-white stash in one piece! The fabric can be used by cutting the stripes into individual strips, but that wouldn't speed up piecing. What if each strip is used as a block? The stripes are 2⅜" wide. By cutting cross-grained strips 2⅞" wide, I will have the tools and inspiration for a black-and-white "Trip Around the World" quilt. Look at all those seams that are already "sewn"!

I needed to add a few more fabrics for background in the corners, then some borders and the ever-present zinger. To add interest to this very large quilt, I selected two different fabrics for the border. One has a larger scale and slightly lighter value. This subtle variation will add dimension to the "frame" of the quilt. Also adding depth are two coordinating background fabrics. The smaller and sharper leaves add clarity and blend into the larger and softer-edged paisley print.

Choosing the zinger was a challenge with this project. Red always works; fuchsia is also good; you can't go wrong with lime green, and a cerulean blue was in the running. All would have been just fine, but when I auditioned a fabric "somewhere between pansy purple and amaranth deep purple," it was more than fine. It was just right.

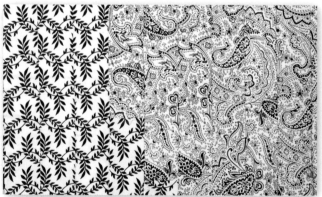

Choosing Border Fabrics

Choosing Background Fabrics

Selecting a Zinger Fabric

CREATING THE QUILT CENTER

Note: The center of the quilt, or the "trip," is created by using two strips of the preprinted fabric for each vertical row. The middle row uses all eighteen fabric squares attached to seventeen fabric squares. Each row is reduced by one fabric, so the center row will have thirty-five squares, the rows on either side of the center will have thirty-three squares, etc.

1 For the vertical center row, lay two $2\frac{7}{8}$" strips of the preprinted fabric end-to-end with the same fabric in the middle. There will always be a center square, with the fabrics going out from the center as mirror images.

2 Remove one square of the center fabric, leaving $\frac{1}{4}$" seam allowance beyond the edge of the second fabric.

3 Stitch the row together and press the seam toward the dark square.

4 Add a $1\frac{1}{2}$" × $2\frac{7}{8}$" zinger strip to each end of the strip. Press the seam toward the zinger.

5 Add a $2\frac{7}{8}$" × 3" white with black leaves background strip to the zinger on each end of the long vertical row. Press the seam toward the zinger.

6 Now that the center row is done, each of the following steps will need to be done for two rows each—one for each side of the center row.

7 Splice each row together by removing an additional fabric each time to create shrinking rows. Splice two rows exactly alike, one for each side of the center row.

8 Add zinger strips to both ends of both rows and press all seams.

9 Add the appropriate background strip to each end of the row by following the chart on page 92. Laying the strips out in cutting order will help keep things flowing and speed up the process. Also, keep strips paired and in order after they have the background strips added and are pressed. We certainly wouldn't want to have to figure anything out later when we are ready to put the vertical rows together!

CREATING THE QUILT CENTER **Step 2**

CREATING THE QUILT CENTER **Step 4**

CREATING THE QUILT CENTER **Step 4**

CREATING THE QUILT CENTER **Step 5**

Number of Squares	Leaf Background	Paisley Background
35	3"	
33	5⅜"	
31	7¾"	
29	10⅛"	
27	12½"	
25	14⅞"	
23	17¼"	
21	19⅝"	
19	22"	
17	24⅜"	
15	18¾"	8½"
13	17⅛"	12½"
11	14½"	17½"
9		33⅞"
7		36¼"
5		38⅝"

10 Create all rows up to the end of the chart. Remember to make two of each row.

11 Make two vertical rows of three squares each by splicing and then adding the zinger strips to each end. Press the seams.

12 Cut out the last fabric square with ¼" seam allowances on both sides and add zinger strips to both ends. Repeat for a second row and press the seams toward the zinger strips. Set these rows aside until it is time to add the borders.

13 Starting once again from the center row, add the next row on each side of the center. There will not be seams to nestle in the center of the quilt, so pin on the fabric lines periodically. This will keep everything in line.

14 It will be possible to nestle the seams of the final squares in each row where the zinger strip has been added. Snug the seams together for clean corners. Sew both rows on and press the seams out.

15 Continue adding the duplicate rows to each side of the growing quilt center. Sew the matching rows to each side and then press the seams out. This methodical approach will help keep the rows in order and reduce confusion. We know I need help with that!

Keep adding rows until all have been joined.

CREATING THE QUILT CENTER Step 12

CREATING THE QUILT CENTER Step 13

MAKING THE RIGHT-HAND BORDER

1 Retrieve a three-square and a one-square row with zinger strips on the ends. Add a 3¾" × 4⅞" strip of the black anemone print to the right edge of the one-square row. Press the seam away from the row.

2 Add a 2⅞" × 6⅛" black anemone print strip to the top of that unit.

3 Add another 2⅞" × 6⅛" black anemone print strip to the bottom of that unit and press the seams out.

4 Add the three-square row to the left edge of that unit.

5 Sew an 8½" × 41" black anemone print strip to the top of that unit, aligned with the zinger strip on the left.

6 Add an 8½" × 41" black anemone print strip to the bottom of the unit. Press the seams out.

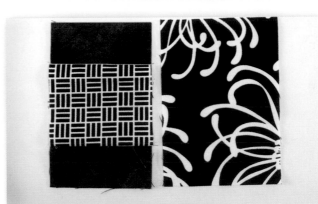

MAKING THE RIGHT-HAND BORDER **Step 1**

MAKING THE RIGHT-HAND BORDER **Step 2**

MAKING THE RIGHT-HAND BORDER **Step 3**

MAKING THE RIGHT-HAND BORDER **Step 4**

MAKING THE LEFT-HAND BORDER Step 5

MAKING THE LEFT-HAND BORDER Step 6

MAKING THE LEFT-HAND BORDER

1 Retrieve the remaining three-square and one-square row with zinger strips on the ends. Add a 3¾" × 4⅞" strip of black with white large dot print to the left edge of the one-square row. Press the seam away from the row.

2 Add a 2⅞" × 6⅛" black with white large dot print strip to the top of that unit.

3 Add another 2⅞" × 6⅛" black with large dot print strip to the bottom of that unit and press the seams out.

4 Add the three-square row to the right edge of that unit.

5 Sew an 8½" × 41" black anemone print strip to the top of that unit, aligned with the zinger strip on the left.

6 Add an 8½" × 41" black with white large dot print strip to the bottom of the unit. Press the seams out.

ADDING THE BOTTOM BORDER

1 Remove the selvages and piece two 8½" black with large white dot strips together, end to end. Press the seam open.

2 Cut the strip to measure 8½" × 74⅛".

3 Sew this piece to the bottom of the quilt and press the seam toward the border.

ADDING THE BOTTOM BORDER Step 3

ADDING THE TOP BORDER

1 Remove the selvages and piece two 8½" strips of black anemone print together, end to end. Press the seam open.

2 Cut the strip to measure 8½" × 74⅛".

3 Sew this strip to the top of the quilt and press the seam toward the border.

ADDING THE RIGHT-HAND BORDER

1 Line up the right border with the right edge of the quilt (with top and bottom borders already added). The center of the border will line up with the last vertical row of the quilt center.

2 Nestle any seams available or pin the edges of the squares periodically to create clean corners. Sew on the right border and press the seam out.

ADDING THE LEFT-HAND BORDER

1 Line up the left border with the left edge of the quilt top, using the block corners in the center of the border to line up with the last vertical row of the quilt.

2 Periodically pin and nestle any available seams to keep the corners neat. Sew on the left border and press the seam out.

FINISHING THE QUILT

1 Add the batting, backing and binding. How easy was that, to finish a "Trip Around the World" in nothing flat! Preprinted fabrics are made to be cut up and used. Have at it!

ADDING THE TOP BORDER Step 3

ADDING THE RIGHT-HAND BORDER Step 2

ADDING THE LEFT-HAND BORDER Step 2

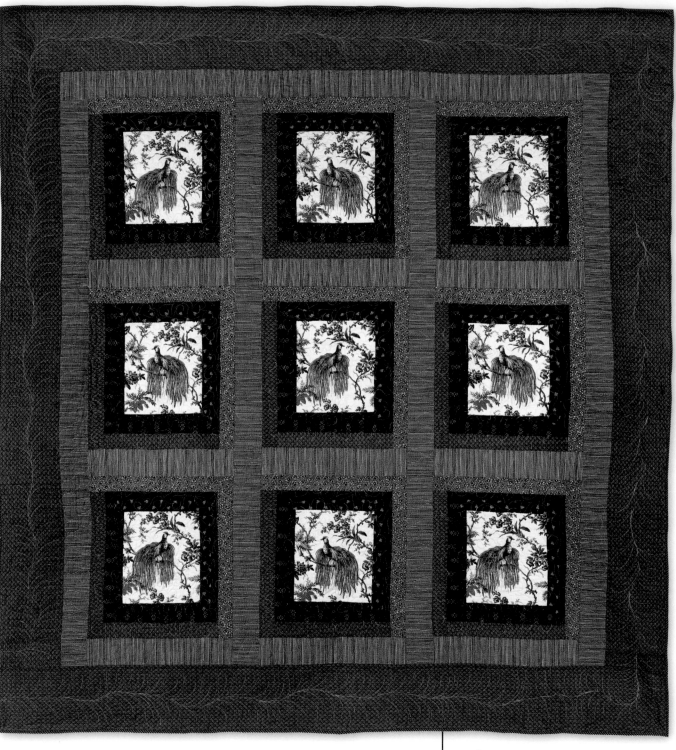

Gentle Morning
88½" × 93"
Pieced and quilted by the author

The colors in this piece are uncharacteristic for me. I tend to shy away from gray, yet in this quilt I have embraced it wholly. The toile calls for subtle hues, so I reached for gray-brown, olive and soft black to enhance the toile and not overpower it. Did I have to go out and shop for these fabrics? Nope. I have sometimes ordered fabric via a picture on the computer screen and I have learned that fabric that appears to be black on the screen is often anything but! Fortunately, for this quilt, I have a supply of such imposters to choose from. The subdued toile became the centerpiece for previously neglected fabrics in my stash. Not only am I going olive green, I'm going "green"!

FABRIC REQUIREMENTS

Pheasant Toile: 9 repeats of the motif, each repeat measuring at least 10½" × 12"

Dark Black Small Print: ⅓ yd.

Dark Olive Print: ⅝ yd.

Dark Black Row Print: ⅝ yd.

Dark Olive with Black Print: ½ yd.

Medium Dark Onion Print: 3⅜ yds.

Medium Leaf Print: ⅞ yd.

Gray Stripe: 2⅝ yds.

Binding: ⅞ yd.

Backing: 8¼ yds.

Batting: 96½" × 101"

CUTTING INSTRUCTIONS

PHEASANT TOILE:
Fussy cut 9 blocks 10½" × 12"

DARK BLACK SMALL PRINT:
Cut 6 strips 1½"; from these strips:
    Cut 9 strips 1½" × 10½"
    Cut 9 strips 1½" × 13"

DARK OLIVE PRINT:
Cut 8 strips 2"; from these strips:
    Cut 9 strips 2" × 11½"
    Cut 9 strips 2" × 14½"

DARK BLACK ROW PRINT:
Cut 8 strips 2"; from these strips:
    Cut 9 strips 2" × 13"
    Cut 9 strips 2" × 16"

DARK OLIVE WITH BLACK PRINT:
Cut 10 strips 1½"; from these strips:
    Cut 9 strips 1½" × 14½"
    Cut 9 strips 1½" × 17"

MEDIUM DARK ONION PRINT:
Cut 10 strips 2½"; from these strips:
    Cut 9 strips 2½" × 15½"
    Cut 9 strips 2½" × 19"
Cut 2 lengthwise strips 9" × 88½"
Cut 2 lengthwise strips 9" × 76"

MEDIUM LEAF PRINT:
Cut 10 strips 2½"; from these strips:
    Cut 9 strips 2½" × 17½"
    Cut 9 strips 2½" × 21"

GRAY STRIPE:
Cut 14 strips 4"; from these strips:
    Cut 9 strips 4" × 19½"
    Cut 9 strips 4" × 24½"
Remove the selvages from the remaining 4" strips, piece them together end to end, press the seams open and from this strip:
    Cut 1 strip 4" × 68"
    Cut 1 strip 4" × 76"

BINDING:
Cut 1 square 29½" for 2¼" continuous bias binding

The Toile Fabric

NOTES ON THIS QUILT

Atypical coloration and a rarely used (by me) method of cutting combine in this design based in tradition. A log cabin block with a very large center calls for fussy-cutting a portion of the toile. Framed with varying sizes and values of logs, the pheasant rests in an understated off-center block. The somber colors evoke a misty morning where pheasants are wandering in the fields. All is hushed and quiet. A sense of expectancy blankets the ground. Wow! A scene like that definitely warrants fussy-cutting!

To determine the size of the center block, the motif needs to be measured. The pheasant will amply fill a block 10" × 11½". That gives enough space to not cramp the bird and allow it space to roam. The gentle value steps of the logs pull the eye outward and create flow within the quilt. Had I used stronger contrasting fabrics, the quilt would have a chunkier, more framed appearance. Also, the quilt would have had the appearance of nine individually framed pheasants instead of the waving meadow created by the subtle value gradations.

The Atypical Colored Fabrics

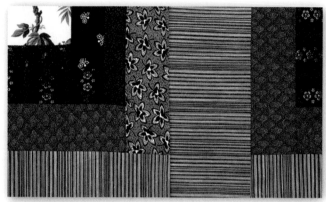
Determining the Size of the Center Block

A Variety of Log Strips

FUSSY CUTTING THE PHEASANTS

1 To fussy cut the centers, use a clear ruler over the design you wish to fussy cut. Cut a 10½" × 12" block.

2 Repeat for a total of five pheasants facing the same direction.

3 This particular print has pheasants facing in two different directions, so I cut out four blocks with the pheasant facing the opposite direction. This surprise adds interest and movement to the quilt.

MAKING THE BLOCKS

1 Line up the precut logs in the order they will be added to the block. Lay a 1½" × 10½" dark black small print log on the bottom of the fussy-cut block, right sides together. Stitch the first log on.

2 Finger press, or use a wooden iron, to press the log back with the seam allowance out.

3 Add a 1½" × 13" strip of the same fabric to the left side of the block, making sure the previous log feeds through the machine first. This keeps the logs going in the correct direction around the center.

4 Finger press, or use a wooden iron, to press the log back with the seam allowance out.

5 Add the 2" × 11½" dark olive print strip in the same manner, feeding the previous log through the machine first. Finger press the log out.

6 Follow with the 2" × 14½" dark olive print strip and finger press the log out.

FUSSY-CUTTING THE PHEASANTS Step 1

FUSSY-CUTTING THE PHEASANTS Step 3

MAKING THE BLOCKS Step 1

MAKING THE BLOCKS Step 2

MAKING THE BLOCKS Step 5

MAKING THE BLOCKS Step 7

MAKING THE BLOCKS Step 9

MAKING THE BLOCKS Step 10

MAKING THE BLOCKS Step 12

7 Start the second log ring with the 2" × 13" dark black row strip. Remember to keep the previous log going through the machine first. Finger press the log out.

8 Continue the ring with the 2" × 16" strip of the same fabric and finger press the log out.

9 Finish this ring by adding the 1½" × 14½" and 1½" × 17" dark olive with black print strips and finger press the logs back.

10 Feeding the previous log into the machine first, stitch the 2½" × 15½" dark onion print strip to the block. Finger press the log back.

11 Follow with a 2½" × 19" strip of the same fabric. Finger press the log back.

12 Complete the final ring with the 2½" × 17½" and 2½" × 21" leaf print strips. Stitch the strips on, then press them out.

13 Repeat Steps 1–12 for all nine blocks.

ADDING THE LATTICE

1 Add a 4" × 19½" gray lattice strip to the bottom of each block. Then, add a 4" × 24½" gray lattice strip to the left side of each block

2 Take the blocks to the ironing board and press all seam allowances out.

ADDING THE LATTICE Step 1

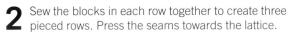
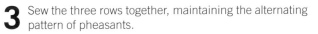

CREATING THE QUILT CENTER

1 Arrange the blocks in rows, alternating the right-facing pheasants and left-facing pheasants.

2 Sew the blocks in each row together to create three pieced rows. Press the seams towards the lattice.

3 Sew the three rows together, maintaining the alternating pattern of pheasants.

4 Stitch the 4" × 68" gray-lattice strip to the top of the quilt center and press the seam out. Stitch the 4" × 76" gray lattice strip to the right side of the quilt center and press the seam out.

ADDING THE BORDER

1 Stitch the 9" × 76" lengthwise border strips to the sides of the quilt. Press the seams out toward the border.

2 Add the top and bottom 9" × 88½" border strips and press the seams out. Another gorgeous quilt top is done!

FINISHING THE QUILT

1 I chose a taupe thread for quilting to keep the piece soft and flowing. I didn't want to darken it by using a black or gray thread.

ADDING THE LATTICE Step 2

2 A free-flowing wreath around the outside is the largest quilting motif. It is next to a slightly smaller-scale licorice whip in the lattice.

3 The block quilting is a smaller-scale leafy vine that encircles the pheasants. All three motifs gradually take the eye in towards the pheasants, just as the fabric choices and blocks do.

4 Everything is gentle and calm except the binding — I couldn't help myself. I just had to add a bias strip for "fencing!"

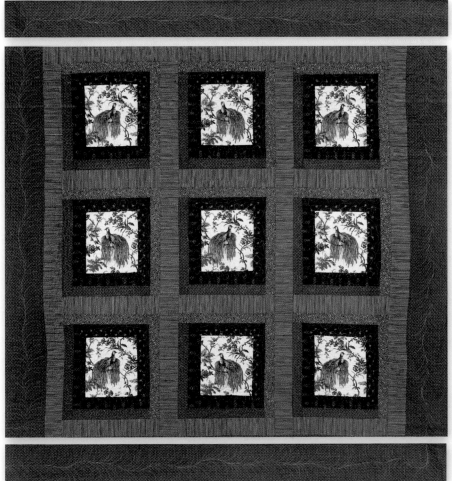

ADDING THE BORDER Step 2

Greet the Day
28¼" × 29"
Pieced and quilted by the author

I call this piece "the little quilt that wouldn't give up." It started with the batik panel, which was so strikingly beautiful all on its own that I didn't want to create anything too ornate or distracting to frame it. I had my own plan for this quilt, but alas, it was not meant to be.

As I auditioned countless fabrics that fit into my plan, niggling away at me was a purple batik in the reject pile that would not leave me alone. An image of it kept popping up in my mind and it wouldn't go away! I did not want to use that fabric—it didn't coordinate with my idea, and I just didn't like it. Frustrated, I finally pulled the purplish obstacle back to the panel. Other purple batiks immediately gravitated toward the panel, and then, click, there it was! The muted and homogenous grouping sang. I gave in to the fabric and ended up creating something more beautiful than I could have imagined.

FABRIC REQUIREMENTS

Batik Panel: at least 21½" × 20½"

Dark Purple Batik: ⅛ yd.

Medium Light Persistent Purple Batik: ¾ yd.

Medium Purple Batik: ⅓ yd.

Darkest Purple Batik: ⅛ yd.

Medium Purple with a Touch of Red Batik: ⅛ yd.

Purple with Black Print: ⅝ yd.

Backing: 1⅛ yds.

Batting: 36¼" × 37"

Sheer Cutaway Nylon Foundation

CUTTING INSTRUCTIONS

BATIK PANEL:
Cut panel to 21½" × 20½"

DARK PURPLE BATIK:
Cut 1 strip 2"
Cut 1 strip 1½"; from this strip:
    Cut 1 strip 1½" × 20"
    Cut 1 strip 1½" × 4½"

MEDIUM LIGHT PERSISTENT PURPLE BATIK:
Cut 2 strips 5"
Cut 3 strips 3"; from one of these strips:
    Cut 2 strips 3" × 4½"
    Cut 1 strip 2" × 4½"
    Cut 2 strips 1¾" × 4½"
    Cut 3 strips 1½" × 4½"
Cut 2 strips 1¼"; from these strips:
    Cut 4 strips 1¼" × 20"

MEDIUM PURPLE BATIK:
Cut 3 strips 3"
Cut 1 strip 1½"; from this strip:
    Cut 1 strip 1½" × 20"
    Cut 1 strip 1½" × 4½"

DARKEST PURPLE BATIK:
Cut 1 strip 2"
Cut 1 strip 1½"; from this strip:
    Cut 1 strip 1½" × 20"
    Cut 1 strip 1½" × 4½"

MEDIUM PURPLE WITH A TOUCH OF RED BATIK:
Cut 1 strip 1½"; from this strip:
    Cut 1 strip 1½" × 20"
    Cut 1 strip 1½" × 4½"

PURPLE WITH BLACK PRINT:
Cut 1 square 18" for 2¼" continuous bias binding

The Original Fabric Grouping

The New and Improved Fabric Grouping

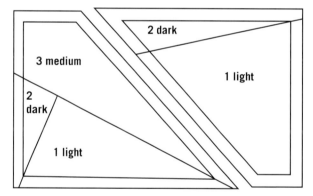
Block A Template
Copy at 250% for full-sized template

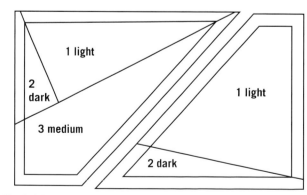
Block A Reverse Template
Copy at 250% for full-sized template

NOTES ON THIS QUILT

When I began pulling fabrics for this piece, I immediately thought of a beautiful gray print fabric I had that ranged from black to the exact purple in the rooster. Gray is a difficult color for me to use—I am not overly fond of it, and I gravitate toward clearer, more defined contrast in my pieces, so this is out of my comfort zone. Nevertheless, I pulled the print from my stash and grabbed a coordinating gray print as well. Next, I tossed in a solid black batik and added two purple batiks. I thought the combination would be perfect. I thought *wrong*. The grouping wasn't singing.

Just then, a purplish batik caught my eye, and though I initially thought, "This is not an attractive piece of fabric," it ended up pulling me in an entirely different direction—one that worked! Once again, I was shown that I need to get out of the way of the fabrics and let them orchestrate themselves. The important lesson learned: I cannot insist on black and white with everything.

To determine the common denominator for this panel, I measured the inside of the panel. Of course, this panel isn't square. The horizontal measurement inside the black border is 20" and the vertical is 19". The black border is 2" on all sides. That doesn't give us an even measurement to work with. The creative process needed to sidestep and figure out the corner blocks of the piece and then fill in with something that would work on both the sides and top and bottom.

I wanted the corner blocks to cap off the ends and not intrude across or down the sides of the quilt, much like old-fashioned picture corners. Dividing the width by four would yield a 5" block, and that would be too cumbersome for the panel. However, when I flipped those numbers and divided the width by five, a 4" block—much more suited to capping off the corners—became my common denominator.

I intended to include a good portion of the black border in the finished piece. However, when the purplish beast won out, the black border needed to shrink to ½" on all sides, acting as a zinger and not a dominant border. Anything wider than that would have destroyed the flow of the quilt.

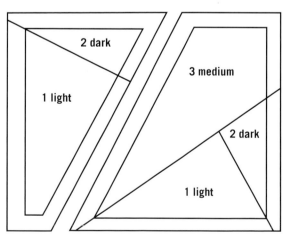
Block B Template
Copy at 200% for full-sized template

CREATING THE CORNER BLOCKS

1 Photocopy and enlarge all of the templates on page 104. Trace two copies of each half of Block A and two copies of each half of Block A Reverse onto sheer cutaway nylon foundation.

After tracing the stitching and cutting lines, write Read Me outside the perimeter of each block half. When stitching, the foundation is right-side up and ready to sew when you are able to read Read Me.

2 Trace eight copies of each half of Block B onto sheer cutaway nylon foundation.

3 Separate all half blocks by cutting them out a bit outside of the traced cutting lines.

4 Keep the Block A, Block A Reverse and Block B half blocks in separate piles.

5 Start with Block A, Side 1 and foundation piece by layering a 2" dark purple strip right sides together with a 5" medium light purple strip underneath the foundation pattern. Have ¼" of both fabrics overlapping into Section 2; stitch along the line between Sections 1 and 2.

6 Trim the seam allowance to ¼" with an Add-A-Quarter ruler. Finger press the fabrics open.

7 Layer the 3" medium light purple strip under the half block with the ¼" seam allowance sticking into Section 3; stitch on the stitching line between Sections 2 and 3. Finger press the fabrics open.

8 Repeat Steps 5–7 for a two Block A, Side 1 half blocks and two Block A, Side 2 half blocks.

9 Press all half blocks well and square them by cutting on the cutting lines.

10 Pin Side 1 and Side 2 of a Block A right sides together, matching the corners. Pin each corner by placing a pin perpendicular to the fabric and through each corner. Sew the seam.

11 Press the seam toward Side 1. Repeat for both Block A blocks.

12 Repeat the entire process to create two Block A Reverse and eight Block B blocks.

CREATING THE CORNER BLOCKS **Step 1**

CREATING THE CORNER BLOCKS **Step 5**

CREATING THE CORNER BLOCKS **Step 6**

CREATING THE CORNER BLOCKS **Step 8**

CREATING THE CORNER BLOCKS **Step 10**

PIECING THE STRIPS Step 1

PIECING THE STRIPS

1 Layer the 1¼" × 20" medium light purple strip, right sides together, with the 1½" × 20" darkest purple strip. Stitch together along the long edge of the strips.

2 Pair a 1¼" × 20" medium light purple strip with a 1½" × 20" dark purple strip and sew together.

3 Pair a 1¼" × 20" medium light purple strip with a 1½" × 20" medium purple with red strip and sew together.

4 Pair a 1¼" × 20" medium light purple strip with a 1½" × 20" medium purple strip and sew together.

5 Press all strip sets with the seam allowance toward the wider strips.

6 Cut four segments 4½" long from each 20" set for a total of sixteen strip-set segments.

CREATING THE BORDERS

1 Lay the strip-set segments to the left of the machine in piles of like fabric.

2 Sew together strip sets of different fabrics to make a double set. Repeat to make a total of seven double sets. Press the seams toward the wider strips. Two single sets will remain.

3 Join two double sets to make a quad set. Repeat for a total of three quad sets. Press the seams toward the wider strips. One double set will remain.

CREATING THE BORDER Step 3

MAKING THE LEFT BORDER Step 6

MAKING THE LEFT BORDER

1 For the left border, line up a 1¾" × 4½" medium light purple strip; a double strip set; a single strip set; a 1½" × 4½" darkest, dark, medium or medium purple with red strip; and another 1¾" × 4½" medium light purple strip. Choose sets with different purple fabrics for variety.

2 Sew the double strip set to the single strip set and press the seam toward the wider strip.

3 Add the 1½" purple strip to the end of the sets and press.

4 Sew a 1¾" × 4½" medium light purple strip to each end of the unit and press. This is the middle of the left border.

5 Cap the left end of the strip with a Block A block.

6 Add Reverse Block A block to the opposite end and press seams toward the strips.

MAKING THE RIGHT BORDER

1 Add a single strip set to a quad set and press the seam toward the wider strip.

2 Sew a purple 1½" strip to the right-side edge of the unit and press the seam toward the purple strip.

3 Finish that end with a 1¾" × 4½" medium light purple strip and press the seam out.

4 Add a 2" × 4½" medium light purple strip to the opposite end and press the seam out. This is the middle of the right border.

5 Cap the right border off with a Block B block on each end and press the seams in.

MAKING THE TOP AND BOTTOM BORDERS

1 Add a 1½" purple strip to the end of both remaining quad sets and press the seam toward the purple strip.

2 Sew a 3" × 4½" medium light purple strip to the left edge of each unit and press the seam out.

3 Complete the middle of the borders with a 1½" × 4½" medium light purple strip to the right-hand edge of the units and press the seams out.

4 Sew a Block B block to the left edge of a Block A block with the point up. Press the seam toward Block A.

5 Repeat Step 4 with another Block B block and a Block A Reverse block with the points down.

6 Add a Block B/Block A unit to the left edge of each border section and press the seams toward the middle.

7 Join the four remaining Block B blocks into two sets with the point creating one point in the middle.

8 Add a Block B unit to the right-hand edge of each border strip and press the seams in.

ADDING THE BORDERS

1 Sew the side border strips to the sides of the panel, keeping the points out. Press the seams toward the panel.

2 Add the top and bottom borders to the quilt, keeping the points out. Press the seams in. Time to quilt your masterpiece!

FINISHING THE QUILT

1 Layer the quilt with batting and backing. I used a cotton batting for a bit of texture, but not any puff. This piece is framed artwork. I didn't want too much loft to distract from the beautiful panel.

2 I utilized the wonderful crackle batik on the panel for quilting inspiration. I followed the crackles to create a marbled appearance that shows off the rooster.

3 Texturizing the rooster was a lot of fun, so I echoed that look in the border with dense straight lines contrasting with curves.

4 By quilting the background a little less closely, it is able to attract your attention by being a little thicker, and yet it immediately shifts the focus to the rooster. I'm not sure how that works, but I'm glad it does! It is as if your eye grabs ahold of the background and slides right into the center.

5 Finishing with a dramatic binding is essential for this piece. The black and purple geometric print gathers all the purples together and anchors them with a touch of black.

MAKING THE RIGHT BORDER Step 5

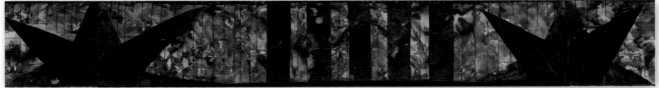

CREATING THE TOP AND BOTTOM BORDERS Step 6

sewplay

SewPlay
28½" × 28½"
Pieced and quilted by the author
Fabrics courtesy of Red Rooster Fabrics

Imagine my excitement when the delightful panel used for this project arrived at my door! The subject matter is darling and the coloration is black and white! Well, almost black and white. Maybe more like black and cream and tan and gray and pink and white. That is close enough for me when the fabrics are so charming!

The panel itself is so strong visually that I hesitated creating too large of a quilt around it. It has strength and interest on its own, and I didn't want to dilute that. The additional small panels were interesting, but the dynamic black border with a button man running on it ended the story for me right there. I needed to focus on that border and show it off without it getting lost in a large quilt.

FABRIC REQUIREMENTS

Preprinted Fabric Panel: At least 20½" × 20½"

Light Stitching Print: ¼ yd.

Black Button Man Print: ½ yd.

Black Stitching Print: ⅓ yd.

Black Button Print: ⅓ yd.

Solid Black: ⅝ yd.

Backing: 1 yd.

Batting: 36" × 36"

CUTTING INSTRUCTIONS

PREPRINTED FABRIC PANEL:
Cut to 20½" × 20½"

LIGHT STITCHING PRINT:
Cut 2 strips 2½"; from these strips:
Cut 2 strips 2½" × 20"
Cut 9 strips 2½" × 4½"

BLACK BUTTON MAN PRINT:
Cut 3 strips 2½"; from these strips:
Cut 2 strips 2½" × 20"
Cut 2 strips 2½" × 4½"
Cut 18 flat-end triangles with an Easy Angle ruler

BLACK STITCHING PRINT:
Cut 3 strips 2½"; from these strips:
Cut 2 strips 2½" × 20"
Cut 9 strips 2½" × 4½"
Cut 2 flat-end triangles with an Easy Angle ruler

BLACK BUTTON PRINT:
Cut 2 strips 2½"; from these strips:
Cut 2 strips 2½" × 20"
Cut 20 flat-end triangles with an Easy Angle ruler

SOLID BLACK:
Cut 1 square 18" for 2¼" continuous bias binding

If an Easy Angle Ruler Is Not Available

BLACK BUTTON MAN PRINT:
Cut 1 strip 3"; from this strip:
Cut 9 squares 3" then cut them in half corner to corner to make 18 half square triangles

BLACK STITCHING PRINT:
Cut 1 strip 3"; from this strip:
Cut 1 square 3" then cut it in half corner to corner to make 2 half square triangles

BLACK BUTTON PRINT:
Cut 1 strip 3"; from this strip:
Cut 10 squares 3" then cut them in half corner to corner to make 20 half square triangles

The Panel

NOTES ON THIS QUILT

Where to begin? The panel measures 20" × 20" to the edge of the red zinger around the button men. Did I want to include some of the cream outside the red? Or even go out into the tan? The strongest spot in the panel is the button man border. I often add zinger borders sandwiched between strong borders, so if I add ¼" around the entire red strip, I won't have to piece a zinger border into the quilt. I like this panel more and more all the time!

While I carefully cut out the panel, I was thinking about a common denominator for this design: 5" goes into 20" four times, but that would make four blocks to a side. I prefer an odd number of blocks. I switched that and reduced it, making 2" my common denominator. I made a checkerboard with 2" squares and then added flying geese. Flying geese are twice as wide as they are tall, so if these blocks are 2" tall, they will be 4" wide; five flying geese blocks will fit on each side. There is my odd number!

Among the coordinating fabrics are three black fabrics of varying but close values. Flying geese with very subtle value changes could frame the panel and add welcome texture. But I don't want the framing to overshadow the button men, so to keep the piece from becoming too dark, in comes the light stitching fabric. It contrasts strikingly with the black fabrics. Used to shift the value placement of the flying geese and checkerboards, the light fabric—along with the black prints—will seamlessly identify a light source for the playroom and keep the quilt from appearing somber.

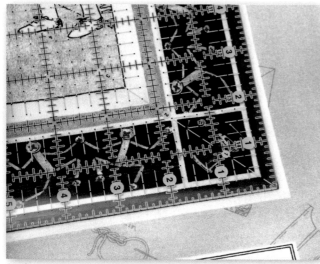

Cutting the Panel

Additional Fabrics

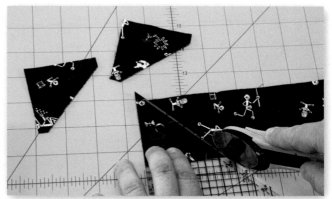

Cutting the Button Man Fabric into Triangles

CONSTRUCTING THE DARK CHECKERBOARD

1 Layer a 2½" × 20" black stitching print strip, right sides together, with a 2½" × 20" black button print strip. Stitch together along a lengthwise edge.

2 Layer a 2½" black stitching print strip, right sides together, with a 2½" black button man strip. Stitch together along a lengthwise edge.

3 Set the seams and press the strips open, with the seam allowance toward the darker strips.

4 Layer the strip sets right sides together; alternating the dark squares, nestle the seam in the middle to prepare for the checkerboard. Cut five segments 2½" wide.

5 Separate the strip sets and cut an additional six segments 2½" wide from the dark stitching print with the black button man print. Layer the segments.

6 Move all layered segments to the left of the sewing machine. Stitch two segments together to create a four-patch block. Repeat for a total of five mixed four-patches and three button man only four-patches.

7 Snip the threads and press the blocks open.

8 Layer two four-patch blocks, with both a button man and button square, right sides together. Keeping the button square in the upper left position, stitch them together. Repeat for a second set of two four-patch blocks.

9 Join the block units and add the last mixed four-patch to make a five-block checkerboard; press all seams one way.

10 Add a four-patch with only button man and black stitching fabrics to each end of the checkerboard and press the seams out. This is the bottom border.

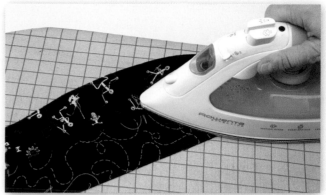

CONSTRUCTING THE DARK CHECKERBOARD Step 3

CONSTRUCTING THE DARK CHECKERBOARD Step 5

CONSTRUCTING THE DARK CHECKERBOARD Step 6

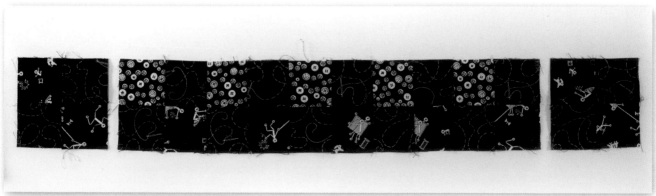

CONSTRUCTING THE DARK CHECKERBOARD Step 10

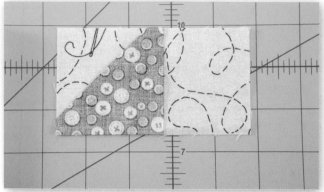

CONSTRUCTING THE FLYING GEESE **Step 1**

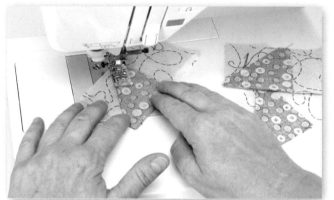

CONSTRUCTING THE FLYING GEESE **Step 2**

CONSTRUCTING THE FLYING GEESE **Step 3**

CONSTRUCTING THE FLYING GEESE

Light Background

1 On a light stitching print rectangle, layer a button triangle on the left side with the blunt triangle ends flush with the top and side of the rectangle.

2 Stitch with a ¼" seam allowance using the left side of the foot to gauge the ¼" seam. Repeat for a total of four blocks.

3 Press the triangle out, keeping the bottom rectangle intact.

4 On these four blocks, place a button triangle on the opposite end of the rectangle, lining up the blunt triangle ends flush with the top and right side of the rectangle.

5 Stitch the triangle ¼" from the diagonal edge of the triangle. Repeat for all four blocks.

6 Press the triangle out flat against the rectangle. Square the blocks to 2½" × 4½" if necessary.

7 Line up two blocks with the triangle in the left block pointing up and the triangle in the right block pointing down to create a ribbon pattern. Sew the blocks together. Repeat for the second set of blocks.

Join the two sets for a row of four button ribbon blocks. Press the seams all in the same direction.

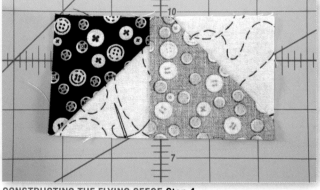

CONSTRUCTING THE FLYING GEESE **Step 4**

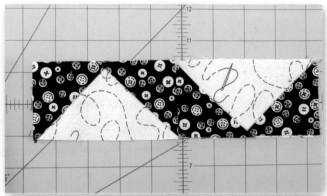

CONSTRUCTING THE FLYING GEESE **Step 7**

8 Repeat Steps 1–6 for five blocks with light stitching print rectangles and button man triangles.

9 Repeat Step 7 for four of these blocks.

10 Add the last block to the left edge of the strip so the beginning and ending blocks both have the triangles pointing down. Press the seams all in the same direction.

Dark Background

1 On a black stitching print rectangle, layer a button triangle on the right side with the blunt triangle ends flush with the top and side of the rectangle.

2 Stitch with a ¼" seam allowance along the diagonal edge of the triangle. Repeat for a total of five blocks.

3 Press the triangle out, keeping the bottom rectangle intact.

4 On these five blocks, place a button triangle on the opposite end of the rectangle, lining up the blunt triangle ends flush with the top and left side of the rectangle. Stitch ¼" from the diagonal edge of the triangle. Repeat for all five blocks.

5 Press the triangle out flat against the rectangle. Square the blocks to 2½" × 4½" if necessary.

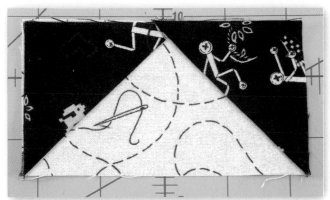

CONSTRUCTING THE FLYING GEESE Step 8

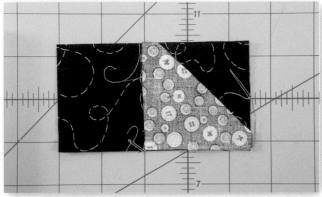

DARK BACKGROUND Step 1

DARK BACKGROUND Step 2

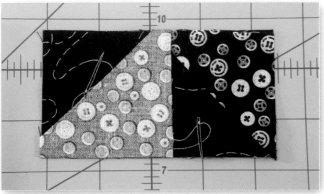

DARK BACKGROUND Step 4

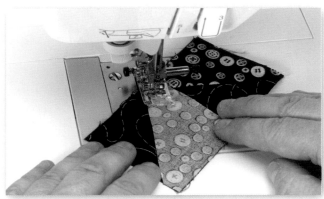

DARK BACKGROUND Step 4

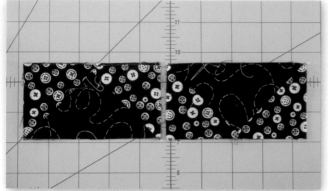

DARK BACKGROUND Step 6

DARK BACKGROUND Step 8

6 Line up two blocks with the triangle on the left pointing up and the triangle in the right block pointing down to create a ribbon pattern. Sew the blocks together. Repeat for the second set of blocks.

Join the two sets for a row of four button ribbon blocks.

7 Add the last block to the edge of the strip so that the beginning and ending blocks both have the triangles pointing up. Press the seams all in the same direction.

8 Repeat Steps 1–6 for four blocks with black stitching print rectangles and button man triangles and press the seams all in the same direction.

Button Man Background

1 On a button man rectangle, layer a black stitching triangle on the right side with the blunt triangle ends flush with the top and side of the rectangle.

2 Stitch with a ¼" seam allowance along the diagonal edge of the triangle and press the triangle out.

3 Place a black stitching triangle on the opposite end of the rectangle, lining up the blunt triangle ends flush with the top and side of the rectangle. Stitch the triangle ¼" from the diagonal edge of the triangle. Press the triangle out flat against the rectangle.

4 Square the block to 2½" × 4½" if necessary.

5 Add the button man block to the left edge of the four-block strip of black stitching background with button man triangles so the triangles are pointing up in the first and last blocks in the row. Press the seams all in the same direction.

6 On the remaining button man rectangle, layer a button triangle on the right side with the blunt triangle ends flush with the top and side of the rectangle. Stitch with a ¼" seam allowance along the diagonal edge of the triangle and press the triangle out.

7 Place the last button triangle on the opposite end of the rectangle, lining up the blunt triangle ends flush with the top and side of the rectangle. Stitch the triangle ¼" from the diagonal edge of the triangle.

8 Press the triangle out flat against the rectangle. Square the block to 2½" × 4½" if necessary.

9 Sew this block to the left edge of the light stitching background blocks with button triangles to complete the ribbon and press the seam.

CONSTRUCTING THE LIGHT CHECKERBOARD

1 Layer a 2½" × 20" light stitching print strip, right sides together, with a 2½" × 20" black button print strip. Stitch together along a lengthwise edge.

2 Layer a 2½" × 20" light stitching print strip, right sides together, with a 2½" × 20" black button man strip. Stitch together along a lengthwise edge.

3 Set the seams and press the strips open with the seam allowance toward the darker strips.

4 Layer the strip sets, right sides together, alternating the dark squares and nestling the seam in the middle. Cut five segments 2½ " wide.

5 Separate the strip sets and cut two additional segments 2½" wide from the light stitching print with black button man print. Layer the like segments with dark squares alternating.

6 Move all layered segments to the left of the sewing machine. Stitch two segments together to create a four-patch block. Repeat for a total of six four-patches. One four-patch block will have two button man squares.

7 Snip the threads and press the blocks open.

8 Layer two four-patch blocks with both a button man and button square right sides together, keeping the button man square in the bottom left position. Stitch them together. Repeat for a second set of two four-patch blocks.

9 Join the block units and add the last mixed four-patch block to make a five-block checkerboard and press all seams one way. This is the right border.

CONSTRUCTING THE LIGHT CHECKERBOARD **Step 1**

CONSTRUCTING THE LIGHT CHECKERBOARD **Step 4**

CONSTRUCTING THE LIGHT CHECKERBOARD **Step 4**

CONSTRUCTING THE LIGHT CHECKERBOARD **Step 9**

CONSTRUCTING THE LIGHT CHECKERBOARD **Step 7**

MAKING THE LEFT AND TOP BORDERS

1 Retrieve the flying geese strips and all remaining blocks. Join the two light stitching background ribbon rows of flying geese blocks together. The button row with one dark background block will be on the bottom with the all-dark block on the left. Stitch the rows together and press the rows open.

2 The light four-patch block with only button man squares goes on the right edge of the light ribbon rows. Sew the block on the end and press the seam out.

3 To complete the top border, add a dark four-patch block with only button man squares on the left end of the ribbon rows. Stitch the seam and press the seam out.

4 Sew together all dark ribbon rows with the button ribbon row ending up on the inside and the button man row on the outside to create the left border. Press the rows open.

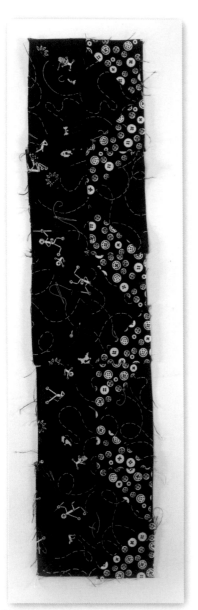

MAKING THE LEFT AND TOP BORDERS Step 1

MAKING THE LEFT AND TOP BORDERS Step 4

MAKING THE LEFT AND TOP BORDERS Step 3

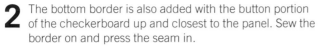

ADDING THE BORDERS

1 With the button ribbon on the inside of the border, sew the left border to the left side of the panel. Press the seam in toward the panel. Likewise, the button portion of the checkerboard right border should be on the inside, closest to the panel. Stitch the border on and press the seam toward the panel.

2 The bottom border is also added with the button portion of the checkerboard up and closest to the panel. Sew the border on and press the seam in.

3 Again, the button portion of the ribbon border is closest to the panel and on the bottom of the top border. Add the border and press the seam in.

FINISHING THE QUILT

1 Layer your quilt with batting and backing. Use simple serpentine crosshatching on the checkerboard borders.

2 Give the ribbon borders a more intricate treatment on the backgrounds to allow the unquilted ribbons to pop up.

3 The panel itself got some outline stitching, stitch-in-the-ditch and additional texturing, especially for the window and rug.

4 Bind *SewPlay*.

ADDING THE BORDERS Step 1

ADDING THE BORDERS Step 1

ADDING THE BORDERS Step 2

ADDING THE BORDERS Step 3

The Gallery

Please enjoy the following quilts and use them as inspiration. They demonstrate additional uses of the Fibonacci sequence and other design ideas covered in the quilt projects. Allow yourself to look at preprinted panels and large scale prints in a new way—they can be the building blocks for unexpected and exciting ideas for future quilts. Large prints can be sliced and diced, vintage panels can be highlighted in contemporary quilts and contemporary panels can be showcased as works of art.

Dig, Dig, Diggety Dig!
45" × 58½"
Pieced and quilted by the author
Fabrics courtesy of Avlyn

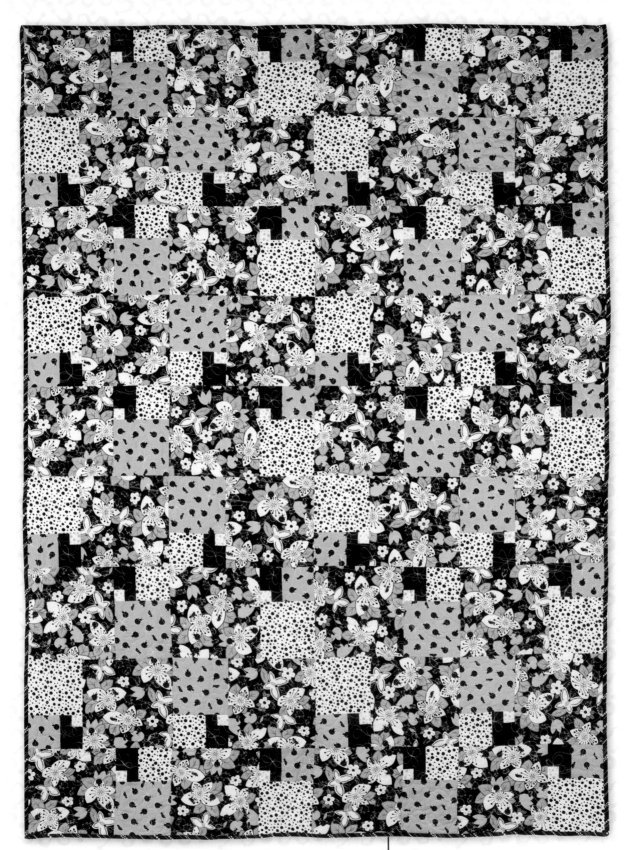

Ladybug Picnic
52½" × 72½"
Pieced and quilted by the author
Fabrics courtesy of Exclusively Quilters

Batik Bouquet
32½" × 32½"
Pieced and quilted by the author

Kangaroo Hop
18" × 21½"
Pieced and quilted by the author

Subtly Stitched
23" × 41"
Pieced and quilted by the author
Fabrics courtesy of Northcott

Art Nouveau Peace
21½" × 41"
Pieced and quilted by the author

Scarlett Radiance
32" × 24"
Pieced and quilted by the author
Fabrics courtesy of Bali Batiks

about the author

Help! Help! I'm caught on the playground and can't get off! Wouldn't that be a wonderful thing? Actually, my life seems somewhat like a playground. During my "real" life, I go to a wide variety of school-sponsored athletic events along with arts events that run the gamut from musicals to speech contests—all that on top of the daily enjoyment of watching my four children turn into productive citizens! In my work life, I travel the country to teach at quilt shows, guilds and quilt shops. Since my students are quilters I don't need to tell you what fun that is! Both of my lives are filled with games and play!

The creative play in this book took me right back to my art classes in elementary and high school. I couldn't wait until the bell rang and it was time to play with texture and fiber. Yarn and jute and cotton cord—yummy! Sculpture soon meshed with fibers and I followed that with creating batik fabric. Whatever will I do with the batik ape I still have hanging in my studio?

The design principles I learned then are mixed with black and white fabrics to form my current design sensibility. I'm so thankful for the solid base I received in public school since I was too afraid to go to art school! I decided then that I couldn't draw so I couldn't go. I've come full circle with fresh eyes and a new understanding of being an artist. I don't need a pencil to draw—I have fabric! Lucky for me my two oldest children are studying art after high school. Maybe they will let me look at their notes!

My kiddoes and he-man are wonderfully flexible. In order to share my love of quilting, I need to be on the road teaching. My adaptable clan fully supports that and frees me to be active in the quilting world as well as very present in their world. I get the best of everything. Perhaps I don't ever want to leave this playground!

It is hard for me to believe that I am sharing my ideas and quilts in my fourth book. It seems like yesterday I drove to the warehouse to pick up a box of copies of my very first book. That initial excitement hasn't waned. This new book has been such a delight to create. It is full of fresh new quilts that have been stuck in my head and longing to get out. Their spots have already been filled with more ideas so I hope you are ready for many more books! I'll continue to travel and teach if you will continue to Breathe, Play, Enjoy! Wave at me on the road, or better yet, invite me to your guild or quilting group—I'd love to share my playground with you. See you soon!

resources

Cross Cuts
www.crosscutsquilting.com
www.crosscuts.cc
crosscuts@springgrove.coop

Bali Fabrics
www.bali-fabrics.com
info@balifab.com

Island Batiks, Inc.
www.islandbatik.com
islandbatik@sbcglobal.net

Marcus Fabrics
Marcus Brothers Textiles, Inc.
www.marcusfabrics.com

Red Rooster Fabrics
www.redroosterfabrics.com

Avlyn
www.avlyn.com
info@avlyn.com

Exclusively Quilters
www.classiccottons.com
customerservice@classiccottons.com

Northcott Silks
Lyndhurst Studio
www.northcott.net
info@northcott.net

Andover Fabrics
www.andoverfabrics.com
info@AndoverFabrics.com

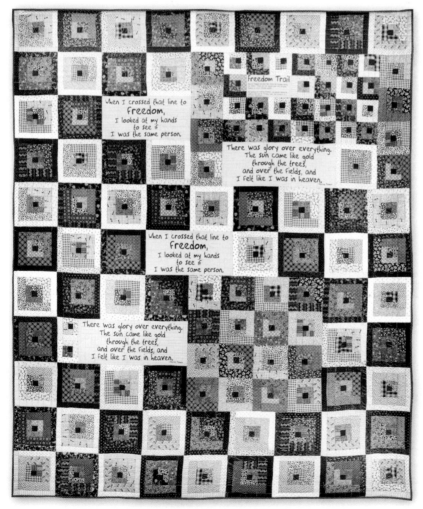

index

Looking for more quilting fun?

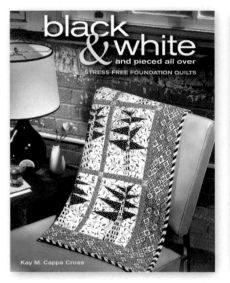

Black & White and Pieced All Over
Stress-Free Foundation Quilts
Kay M. Capps Cross

The method used in this book for making black-and-white, foundation-pieced quilts is unlike any other paper-piecing book on the market: it's stress-free. You will be able to achieve precision and perfect points without even trying!

paperback; 8¼" × 10⅞"; 128 pages
ISBN-10: 0-89689-942-X
ISBN-13: 978-0-89689-942-1
SRN: Z3659

Appli-Curves
Elaine Waldschmitt

Perfect curves can be created every time with this simple technique. This book includes 12 gorgeous projects and a bonus CD with 20 appliqué templates.

paperback; 8¼" × 10⅞"; 128 pages
ISBN-10: 0-89689-601-3
ISBN-13: 978-0-89689-601-7
SRN: Z1659

Big-Print Quilts
15 Projects Using Large-Scale Fabrics
Karen Snyder

Use beautiful and novelty large-scale fabrics for quilting without fear! Karen Snyder leads you through 15 projects for all skill levels.

paperback; 8¼" × 10⅞"; 128 pages
ISBN-10: 0-89689-481-9
ISBN-13: 978-0-89689-481-5
SRN: Z0745

These and other fine Krause Publications titles are available from your local craft retailer, bookstore or online supplier, or visit our Web site at www.mycraftivitystore.com.